AN OCEAN OF THOUGHTS

ONE MAN'S JOURNEY
FROM SELF-DESTRUCTION TO SELF-REALIZATION

Hawkeye Publishers

An Ocean of Thoughts:
One Man's Journey from Self-Destruction to Self-Realization

For more information, please address Hawkeye Publishers
HawkeyePublishers.com

Library of Congress Control Number: 2018949281

Paperback: 978-1946005243
Hardcover: 978-1946005250
Ebook: 978-1946005267

SECTION I

NEW JERSEY

CHAPTER 1

When I woke up that morning, emerging from a dream I can no longer remember, I found myself snuggled with a pillow, not with my ex-girlfriend, Melissa. Familiar feelings of disappointment and loneliness came over me as I willed myself out of bed to start the day as I usually did back then, by getting high. As I breathed in, seagulls glided past my window, and the steady sound of traffic pervaded my space from the street outside.

After my wake and bake, I sat on the sofa staring straight ahead with a cup of coffee, waiting for my roommate and best buddy, Jon, to get up. We lived in a rundown garden apartment in the West End, just three blocks from Junk Beach. He still hadn't gotten up by the time I finished my coffee, so I decided to walk down to the beach. Standing on the Long Branch boardwalk, leaning against a metal railing, I looked out at the ocean, and couldn't help but feel like a loser.

I'd been feeling that way for the last two years. I'd grown up in ritzy Colts Neck, about 12 miles west of the West End, where success was expected of us. And though I'd graduated from college two years ago, I still just worked as a delivery boy at my family's pizza joint, where I'd been on and off since I was 14. This was a bitter disappointment. I had higher expectations for my life, though I wasn't exactly sure what they were.

I didn't want a white-collar career, but I sure as hell didn't want to spend the rest of my life working at Skinny Vinnie's. I wanted to live an unconventional and non-materialistic life while still somehow enjoying the comfortable lifestyle I'd grown up with. At that point in my life, though, I hadn't yet realized how difficult it would be to have it both ways. Standing there on that boardwalk, I had no realistic vision for my future. I was just stoned.

A happy-looking young couple holding hands walked by on the beach below. I tried to resist feeling down about getting dumped nearly 18 months ago, but it was hard to forget that I hadn't even been on a date since Melissa decided to move on. Melissa was smart, good-looking, and way too successful to have a guy like me as her boyfriend. There I was, in my black Converse high tops, faded Levi's, and pocket T-shirt delivering pizzas. She waited a while for me to catch up to her, but I was stuck. She didn't want to keep living with her parents in Oakhurst, taking the train into the city for work, but I wouldn't commit to getting an apartment in Red Bank with her. There was no way I could hold on to her.

Jon greeted me when I walked in our front door, "Hey Joppa, want some breakfast?" He was at the stove, cooking up a mound of corned beef hash and eggs, dyed green for St. Patty's Day. We scarfed down breakfast and followed it with a six-pack each, then made our way down to the St. Patty's Day parade in Belmar. The parade, easily one of the Jersey Shore's best, was a rowdy affair, and it only worked up our thirst, so we hung around Belmar after it was over, hitting the pubs for a few more beers, then we returned home to get high and hang around until Jon had to work his early shift at Skinny Vinnie's. We planned to continue celebrating this blessed Irish holiday with further inebriation at the end of his shift. Sure, neither of us had an ounce of Irish blood coursing through our veins, but it was a great excuse to drink. Not that we needed one.

Drinking had become less of an adventure for us in our twenties, like it had been when we were high school kids sneaking beers. Now it was a way of life, or, more accurately, a buffer from real life, filled with camaraderie and periodic oblivion. We spent large parts of our days, and nights, drunk. When we were bored, which was most of the time, we'd go get a case of beer and say, "Let's make something happen." At least once a week, that something was blowing our money at the local strip joint, where we'd sit with our pals, get smashed, and slip into lusty trances. There was no need to keep conversations going with each other, nor did we have to try to be witty or interesting with the girls. Not much thought or effort was required, which was how I liked to live my life back then. But it was also degrading for all of us involved. We guys sat there mostly in silence, pretending to have a good time, all the while knowing that this was the only way we could see a woman half-naked.

When Jon went to work that night, I went with him and hung around the kitchen, sipping rum and cokes and helping our coworker Roy throw pizzas into the oven. A phone order came in from Mr. Schaeffer, one of our regular customers who also bought weed from the drivers. Jon took the call and I decided to go along on the delivery with him. After placing the pie in its warmer bag on the backseat, Jon threw me the keys to the Blue Rose, jumped into the passenger seat, pulled out his one-hitter, and took a suck.

Mr. Schaeffer lived ten minutes away, over on Joline Avenue, in a predominantly black neighborhood by the Monmouth Park horse track. When we got to his house, I waited in the car with the engine running while Jon made the delivery. Seconds later, I saw something moving fast out of the corner of my eye. It was Jon running down the driveway with some guy chasing after him. Jon jumped into the passenger seat, barely shutting the door as I slammed the car into reverse. I screeched down Joline Avenue, burning rubber. Seconds later, the stranger who'd been chasing Jon pulled up behind us in a Crown Victoria. Out of sheer panic, I crashed Jon's Mustang into a grove of trees along a median right before the toll booth for the Garden State Parkway.

We jumped out of the car and started to run, but the stranger and three cop cars pulled up with sirens blaring and lights spinning, and they all sprung from their cars with guns pointed at us. We froze.

It turns out, the stranger was actually Schaeffer's brother, a state trooper who was visiting him at the time of the pizza delivery. When Schaeffer opened the door, Jon presented him, as was usual, with a box of pizza along with a half-ounce bag of "Mauie Wowie" on top of it. Schaeffer's eyes got wide and he shook his head in a panic, but his brother had already seen what went down, and instantly he was pushing past Schaeffer and chasing after Jon, who'd immediately started running at the site of the badge.

As we sat in the back of one of the police cars, handcuffed and freaking out, the cops wrote us up tickets for marijuana possession, and intent and conspiracy to distribute, plus a whole swath of moving violations including speeding, careless driving, reckless driving, drunken driving, eluding a New Jersey state trooper, and attempting to leave the scene of an accident. Then we were taken to jail and booked. Sitting in the holding cell that night, wondering how my life could possibly get worse, I wished that Jon and I were back in high school, at the Billy Martin Clubhouse. Those were much simpler times.

CHAPTER 2

Ah, the Billy Martin Clubhouse, my old refuge. It was a treehouse in my backyard, way out in the middle of the woods. Jon and I and a few other friends would hang out there in our early teens, listening to music, smoking, drinking, and talking endlessly. We were diehard Yankee fans, particularly of their scrappy manager Billy Martin. He was ballsy and crazy, the type of guy who would stick up for you if you were his buddy no matter how wrong you were, and would keep fighting no matter how bad his ass was getting kicked. He was the perfect guy for some Jersey kids to name their hangout after.

My friendship with Jon Salonica marked the beginning of my teen years. Jon had moved to Colts Neck when we were in middle school, and we lived on the same street back then. He was generally quiet and a good student, but he had a defiant side. You could say he had a chip on his shoulder. He either loved you or hated you, and when he loved you, he was extremely loyal. He was slow to warm up, but once he did, there was no turning back — he was your friend for life. If he hated you — well, he'd already been in a couple fistfights.

His father was a Greek businessman, and his mother was a Jewish housewife. His dad did not like to take risks, socially or financially. He was content living a buttoned-down life. After studying business at Rutgers, he went to work for Merrill Lynch in Manhattan his whole adult life, taking the 75-minute train ride to work early each weekday from Matawan. Jon was a lot like his dad in a lot of ways, though he didn't like to admit it. They were both wiry with curly black hair and a natural aptitude for business and numbers. But Jon adamantly did not want to be like his dad. Instead, like me, he dreamed of living a bohemian lifestyle, like as an artist or musician — except that he didn't have any artistic talent. His dad wasn't that bad, though. On Jon's 17th birthday, he gave him a '68 Mustang convertible that had *The Blue Rose* painted in a flourish of cursive across its trunk. We laughed about it, but Jon left it there, and from that moment on, we only referred to his Mustang as the Blue Rose.

We hung out for the first time during our freshman year of high school. I was lifting weights one afternoon in my garage when I noticed Jon and his dad parked out front in their Coupe de Ville, the engine running and the two of them fighting inside. Suddenly, Jon bolted out of the car, slamming the door behind him, and stormed off, looking like he was about to cry. I called out to him, asking him if he could spot me while I was benching. We ended up talking about girls, music, everything, and when I was done lifting, we sparked up a joint and listened to Pink Floyd. We were fast friends, best friends.

CHAPTER 3

Skinny Vinnie's wasn't much to look at from the outside — just a corner brick building with a small parking lot — but it was popular, with full tables and bar every night. The inside hadn't changed much over the years. The tables were covered in thick white tablecloths. Maps of Italy and paintings of the Italian countryside adorned the walls. A large Yankee Stadium mirror was next to the TV over the bar. Uncle New's office was way in the back of the restaurant, down a twisting hallway. That's where Jon and I waited anxiously as my uncle, talking intently on the phone with a police captain he knew, tried to get us out of our recent jam. He sat at his desk, looking away from us, forehead wrinkled. Roy was there, too, across the room from me and Jon. We were all nervous and fidgeting. My mind was racing. Roy had his head in his hands, resting his elbows on his knees, and occasionally ran his fingers through his hair or patted his beard down. Jon just looked scared shitless with a nervous smile plastered on his face. I imagine I looked about the same as him. If anyone could get us out of this, though, it was New.

Rumors had always circulated that my uncle was connected. New didn't confirm or deny this. We were never sure just how legitimate his business was. No one remembers him ever being arrested for anything, so he was either on the level or really good at his racket.

We just considered him to be a minor gangster and left it at that. He'd migrated to the Shore about 20 years ago, after inheriting some money, and bought Skinny Vinnie's. He traded up from an apartment in the Down Neck section of Newark to a high-rise condo with a boat slip in upscale Monmouth Beach. Everyone called him Newarky, and I shortened it to New. I'm the only one who calls him that. He was my mom's brother, and my dad's best friend, before my dad died, back when I was five years old.

Sitting there in New's office waiting to see if he could fix our mess, it felt as though the world was standing still and I was looking at everything from the outside. Roy, Jon, and I exchanged worried glances. Roy didn't even need to be here. It was his day off, but he was worried about us. Sure, Roy would join in on our antics sometimes, but he was older and had been around the block. He'd try to steer us in the right direction, saying if we detoured, life would happen to us. I guess this was the type of thing he meant. There are crossroads every day where we can make mistakes or improve our lives, depending on our character and the quality of our judgment, but certain events and certain days seemed more significant. That day was one of them. Looking back, it marked my transition into true adulthood.

New hung up the phone hard. I looked up, and he was expressionless. He didn't say anything at first, just crumpled up a White Castle hamburger bag that was on his messy old desk, then tossed it into a big metal

New York Giants trash can across the room. He slowly looked over at us and told us straight out what the deal was. No lecture, no jokes. He started with Jon's punishment: He'd have to do community service and be on probation for two years. Okay, not bad. Then he got to me.

"You were the driver, and you were drunk," he said. "So, you get community service, too, but you also have to go live in a halfway house for the next few months and go to Alcoholics Anonymous meetings. You'll have your court date, lose your license for a while, and you'll have to pay a bunch of fines."

He drew a puff from his cigar and continued, "This won't go away. I'll keep working on it, and I'll give you more details as it gets worked out." He then looked up, glancing over my shoulder out the window by the door, and grinned. "One of the other details is about to knock on the door."

Sure enough, a second later, there were two quick raps on the door. I got up and opened it, and stood face to face with a middle-aged man in a sailor's uniform that was adorned with a whole mess of ribbons. New introduced me to BM1 Stallworth, the local recruiter, then said goodbye to us both. Stallworth led me out to his car, and as he started it up, he said, "I'm taking you to a rehab house over in Ocean Grove." Uncle New had managed to get me into The Last House on the Block recovery home, and, as we drove, Stallworth told me I'd been accepted into the navy's Delayed Entry

Program for a three-year enlistment. After my 90 days in rehab, I would go to boot camp, and then I'd be off to sea, aboard a ship in San Diego or Norfolk, or maybe even Pearl Harbor.

Everything had happened so fast. New had been working on this for the past few days, trying to find a way out of jail time for me, and then my entire life changed within seconds. The day before, I was a pizza delivery boy who'd just got a DUI. Now, I was sitting in a car being driven to a halfway house by a sailor who was signing me up for a stint in the navy. And oddly enough, as I sat there, I felt a certain freedom come over me. No more worrying and no more floundering. In an odd way, it felt good to bottom out and begin a new phase.

CHAPTER 4

I slept late that first morning at rehab, then I just laid there, thinking. How did I wind up here? A man in his twenties has an open, forked road ahead of him, and the course he chooses will greatly impact the rest of his life. Those years can be the foundation for cementing a career and looking toward starting a family. I spent this crucial time loafing and partying, avoiding responsibility. A while back, Roy had warned me about this. He said this extension of my adolescence would be something I'd spend my thirties paying for. "If you're lucky," he said, "by the time you reach your forties and get back on track, you can glorify those dark days as being wild. You'll be known as a colorful character who settled down." He continued, "Settling down successfully is a matter of timing. Some people get married, pop out a bunch of kids, and buy homes prematurely. Other people drift forever and miss the career and family boat. Of course, there are those who do everything at the right time and have a great life. It's one of life's major judgment calls."

And my poor judgment had led me here, to The Last House on the Block. Which, by the way, wasn't really the last house on the block — there was one more house between here and the beach. But it was called that because going into recovery is the last stop before winding up dead, in jail, or at a nuthouse.

Last House was run by a scrappy little guy called Saint. He was an ex-sailor and embodied all the stereotypes of an old salty dog. He had a salt-and-pepper crew cut and a little mustache, and he was completely covered in tattoos, most of which were images of wild beasts baring their teeth or wild women baring their breasts. There was a big anchor with the letters "USN" on his left forearm, and on his right was the Tasmanian devil cartoon character. And, shit, he could cuss a blue streak. But, despite his gruff exterior, he was also a tender, funny, and thoughtful person who would do whatever he could for the guys staying at the home.

Saint ran the place like a navy ship, busting his balls to keep it running tight. He worked hard and expected the same from everyone else. He'd take you in, but if you broke the rules, you were immediately kicked out. He didn't play any games. No favorites were shown and no rules were bent. Newcomers were usually overwhelmed, and they often felt like victims. They'd grumble that they'd hardly done anything wrong and that the world was against them. Saint wouldn't take any of that. I remember a new resident, James, who almost caused a head-on collision with a full school bus while driving drunk. One morning at a house meeting, he started whining that his punishment was unfair — the guys he'd been drinking and driving with that day not only didn't get busted, but they also managed to keep their jobs and their girlfriends. Saint snapped, "Just be grateful you didn't get what you deserved!

If you're looking for sympathy, you'll find it between *shit* and *syphilis* in the dictionary." Then, he added, "Sometimes you get what you want. Sometimes you get what you need. And sometimes you just get what you fucking get." That was sort of Saint's motto, so much so that he had it written on a plaque that hung down in the basement where he liked to do AA step work. Those were pretty good words to live by.

There was a strange collection of oddballs at the house, roughly a dozen at any given time. Our shared goal was 90 days of sobriety, then we'd head to either a longer-term halfway house or somewhere else where we could reliably try to stay sober. Employment, house meeting attendance, and chores for the upkeep of the place were all required.

By far the most interesting guy at the house was Byron, a vibrant gay black man in his fifties who was basically Saint's right-hand man. He'd been there for years, and his carefree spirit counterbalanced Saint's steady hand. Originally from a Jewish neighborhood in Brooklyn, with a mother from North Carolina, his charisma lit up a room and he could charm the roughest dude from the ghetto, the stuffiest starched-shirt from the suburbs, or the most racist hick from the sticks. Hell, he could even make old brooding Saint laugh out loud. But a lifetime of drinking had damaged his liver, and it was hard for him to get around. Sometimes when he'd laugh too hard, he'd erupt into coughing fits. It was sad to see someone with such an energetic personality be so physically restricted, but his lust for life shined through, and it was contagious. I always made sure to stop and chat with him while he rocked on the porch in the evenings after supper, where he held court with newcomers to the house and old-timers from the AA clubhouse. He'd listen to what newcomers had to say before replying with something like "pray on it" or some other overworked AA phrase. Rather than offering advice, Byron got the newcomers to work it out for themselves. He was the unofficial, unpaid counselor of the house. He was easy to admire.

Vodka John, another long-time resident at Last House, was my most enigmatic housemate. A ruddy-faced, macho weightlifter in his forties, he supposedly had ten years of sobriety and he could quote whole sections from the "Big Book" verbatim. When he wasn't at the house, you could find him at the AA club across from the beach in Belmar, hanging around and chasing women new to the program. The club had four or five meetings each day in the back room, and members could hang around the clubhouse all day if they wanted to. That's exactly what Vodka John would do, and that was pretty much the opposite of what you hoped to accomplish after sobering up. People in the program had mixed feelings about him. He was loud and a braggart, and it seemed like his personal growth had stalled out. But he was also a favorite among the newcomers, and for good reason. He'd been through it and he had a lot of wisdom to share. He was relatable. John brought in a lot of new recruits and helped shepherd them through their first few days or weeks, depending on how long they lasted.

One thing he said to me early on was, "You're right where you're supposed to be." Those words really hit me, and I returned to them often as I struggled to accept my situation and find gratitude in my life. Another time, as I was complaining about where I was in life, saying, "I wish I could have sobered up years ago." He shook his head. "Nah, you can't regret the past," he told me. "Not only can you not change it, but it's your greatest asset. It took each screw up, bust, wrong move, failure to act, and every humiliation along the way to bring you to the place you're at today. The trick is to remember that, so that you don't decide to take a drink or go back to drugs later on." I nodded.

Probably the most irritating guy at Last House was Lance. He was just miserable. He seemed like the kind of guy who had no friends and, if he weren't at Last House, he'd still be living with his mother. He was always complaining, always irritated by one thing or another. Plus, he was a snitch — you couldn't make a mistake in that house without Saint hearing about it from Lance. He'd been living at Last House forever, but he still hadn't gotten his life together. He went to AA, NA, GA, Al-Anon, and whatever other 12-step programs you could think of, but everyone at Last House still suspected that he drank regularly, with the bums under the Asbury boardwalk. The weirdest thing about Lance was that he lived at Last House by choice. He didn't have orders to be there, and he worked a few days a week as an electrician, which gave him enough money to be able to afford his own place. I think he just needed the company.

We got a new guy, Jericho, a few weeks after I moved in. He was a local boy a few years younger than me whose family was big in area politics. That guy had a huge chip on his shoulder. There was an old AA adage that you can't be too dumb to get AA, but you can be too smart for it. Jerry thought he was too smart for it. He was at the house only a couple of weeks, maybe, and then decided he could do better on his own and took off. A few weeks later, he was on the front page of the *Asbury Park Press*. He'd killed his girlfriend, throwing her off his boat anchored a few miles off the coast near Manasquan. Then he sat down in a chair at the tail end of the boat and slit his wrists with a fishing knife, bleeding to death. The fishing pole was in the holder beside him, with the fishing line still in the water.

I wasn't close to him. He was just one of many faces that came and went at the house, but it troubled me nonetheless that he'd started the program and it didn't help him. I brought it up to some of the guys at the house while we were in the kitchen cleaning up after breakfast. Saint shrugged his shoulders. "Not everybody makes it in AA," he said.

"Yeah, some people come and go," Byron added. "They don't stick around because they weren't done drinking and messing up their lives yet. Some come back. Some just disappear. And you never know if they'll resurface again in AA. They might go back out and drink for their rest of their lives, and sometimes they meet some horrible end. It's just a fact of life."

Vodka John agreed. "Others die so we can remember how bad this disease is," he said. "So we can appreciate what we have."

Saint started to say that not everyone who walks through the doors of AA gets better. But then I interrupted him with, "I thought—"

He cut me off, barking, "You're still a newcomer, Joppa. You've got a broken thinker. Remember: Your best thinking landed you at this halfway house. So take the cotton out of your ears and learn from us old-timers, like Jericho should've done."

My face fell. His sudden harshness hurt, and he could see it in my face. He softened his delivery: "We're all crazy here."

"Luckily, we aren't all acting crazy on the same day," Byron interjected.

CHAPTER 5

Part of my recovery plan was to attend AA meetings. In AA, paradox abounds. I'm supposed to look at myself honestly, but not be self-obsessed. According to step one, I am powerless, yet I need to change everything about myself and live completely differently. I must learn to rely upon a power greater than myself, clean house, make amends, maintain spirituality, and help others. That's a tall order. I wanted to move forward, but I also didn't want to pretend as if my life had started only after I reached recovery. A common refrain in AA is to take it one day at a time, so I guessed that was what I was going to have to do.

AA taught me how to live, and it became my social life. Hell, it became my world. My life seemed to be one big meeting. When I wasn't at a meeting, I was focused on gathering material to share at the next one. I volunteered with one of the Asbury Park Salvation Army meetings every week, brewing coffee before the meeting and helping clean up after it. I also gave my phone number out to some of the other attendees so they could call me when they needed help. I liked that anyone could come to meetings — people from all walks of life, all classes — even people who weren't alcoholics, like those with mental illnesses, social issues, major life problems. AA was an accessible form of group therapy for me, filled with misfits I could relate to.

A few times a week, all of us at Last House would pile into the van and head off to the Salvation Army or another local meeting. We'd all take our turns sharing. I wanted to be philosophical and funny and impress everyone else with my shares, but every time I planned out what I thought was a witty or profound share, it fell flat. Byron tended to tell the same stories over and over. I genuinely liked the guy, but how was telling the same old story helpful for anyone? At least my stories were funny, even if I seemed to be the only one who thought so.

At the Salvation Army, a lot of the residents who attended the meetings were one step away from living on the street, and most of them were mentally ill to some degree. Homeless people would often wander into our meetings, take a few donuts and a cup of coffee, then wander back out, though occasionally they'd stay and listen, and sometimes tell an incoherent, rambling story. During the meetings, Salvation Army workers would check in on us a few times a night, I think for our protection. Admittedly, some of our new residents at Last House weren't particularly stable either, but I thought most of us guys from Last House were much better off than the guys at the Salvation Army, even though we too were down on our luck.

I first met Corners at the Salvation Army meetings. He was actually a former tenant of Last House, but

Saint had kicked him out before I got there. He was a low-bottom drunk, a chronic relapser who, unlike Lance, had actually been caught drinking. Corners got his name because he was known to desperately slurp the last little sips of booze that pool up in the "corner" of a liquor bottle when it's tilted. He came to meetings sporadically, always dressed in rags, always with a colorful story to tell. One night, he told us that he was a victim of voodoo, specifically from his magic prayer beads. "I prayed to meet women," he said, "and those 'pussy beads' made it happen. I was getting laid left and right — all ages, good looking, bad looking. All kinds of women. And you know what? It was a curse. These women made massive drama for me. They were either complete nut-jobs, stole from me, or their husbands were hunting me down all over town. I took those beads, corked them in a wine bottle, and threw it off the Asbury boardwalk into the ocean. I've been doing fine since." Except he clearly hadn't. The night he told that story, he was hunched over and looked more disheveled than ever — it was the last night I saw him at a meeting, and I wasn't sure what happened to him. I felt sorry for him, but I also felt superior to him. I wasn't that bad off — I was just a minor drunk.

On the other side of the coin were the meetings we went to in Sea Girt, a conservative, snobby beach town. At one of the meetings, a woman shared a story about her dying cat. "Cadillac problems," I thought to myself. Saint had come along with us to this meeting, and he caught me rolling my eyes. Later, back at the house, he came out as I was sitting on the porch and said, "Hey, Joppa, keep the focus on you. There's no need for you to take other people's inventories. We can all relate to the feelings that other people have, even if we can't relate to the events. Even if you think Byron or Vodka John are full of crap, that crap might sound good to a newcomer. Maybe that newcomer would get something out of it and decide to keep coming around instead of writing off AA and pissing his life away. Principles before personalities, okay?"

They say that desperation leads you to AA and tolerance keeps you there. It's true. While I was judging other folks at meetings for their stories that I didn't think were profound enough, or who had major issues beyond just alcoholism, doubting many of them would ever get better, I was feeling superior to them. But Saint was right. Invariably, I would hear something that I could relate to at a meeting and all my feelings of superiority would dissolve. And if something I heard didn't personally affect me, it might affect someone else. I learned that AA isn't a performance, and it isn't about impressing people. I came to understand that the most appreciated and thought-provoking shares were the honest, spontaneous ones that came straight from the heart. It didn't matter if it was a good story, or some profound statement. Those shares are the ones that help the speaker and everyone else in the room the most. And that was the point of it.

CHAPTER 6

I'd been at Last House a month, getting used to AA, adjusting to my new life, and growing closer to my housemates. I felt I had a good foundation in AA and at the house, and I felt more hopeful than I had when I entered the program a month before. I was beginning to think about getting a sponsor and starting the AA step work. Saint had suggested I write out my drinking history, and it was immediately apparent when I finished that I was a problem drinker right from the start. I was my own worst enemy. I was always fighting against myself: my limitations, obstacles, perceived failures. I was just trying to find happiness and my place in life, but I was fighting reality every step of the way. That was my true challenge, I realized. I needed to accept reality and find fulfillment in ordinary living. Like Roy used to say, I was "learning to live with my dragons."

One of my probation requirements was to do 300 hours of community service, and after I settled in at Last House, I got set up with a position at Sandy Hook refurbishing old buildings, cleaning up the beaches, and doing whatever else needed to be done. Part of the National Parks System, the Hook was the northernmost beach on the Atlantic in New Jersey. It had a special place in my heart — it was one of the first beaches where I tried surfing, before I realized

I couldn't surf worth a damn. I was excited to get to work there.

The night before my first shift, I went out for a walk to the boardwalk, as had become my routine, to get a newspaper after supper. Reading the paper made me feel like I was doing something normal — something people who weren't in recovery did as a regular part of their everyday lives. But, perhaps more importantly, it also gave me time away from the house to think, uninterrupted.

The newspaper box was at the northern edge of the boardwalk by the Paramount Theatre in front of Convention Hall. After I purchased the paper, I folded it over, tucked it under my arm, and instead of simply heading back to Last House, I made my way to a spot behind the old theatre. I was surprised to find a man who was maybe 10 years older than me, with a beard and a wild mess of salt-and-pepper curls, sitting on the boardwalk in a cross-legged meditation pose.

Sensing my presence, he turned around, smiled at me, and motioned for me to join him. I sat next to him, cross-legged, and we gazed out at the dark ocean together. Lights beamed down on the beach, highlighting the waves. We sat there a long time without talking. I'd never meditated before, and I wasn't really sure what I was doing, but it was so peaceful I completely lost track of time. I glanced at my watch and saw it was later than I'd expected. I got up to leave and he looked up at me, smiled, put his hands into a prayer gesture, and bowed slightly. I awkwardly did the same. Then I jogged down the boardwalk, my paper folded under my arm.

The next morning, Vodka John drove me up to the Sandy Hook ranger station to check in for my first shift. As I walked up to the office, my jaw dropped when I saw the park ranger working inside. It was the very same dude from the boardwalk the night before! He grinned as I walked up, as if he knew my story and had been eagerly awaiting our reunion.

His name was Silver, and once I was checked in and done with my orientation, he and I drove out to the beaches, chatting easily. When I mentioned the odds of us meeting the night before, he told me, "I meditate there every night on my way home. You're welcome to join me." I asked him how he got into meditation, and he said he was initially exposed to it when he read *The Dharma Bums* by Jack Kerouac and *Siddhartha* by Herman Hesse.

"I was getting into Eastern philosophy at the time and I wanted to get more into writing, so I went to this summer writing program at the Naropa Institute, a school in Boulder, Colorado, that was founded by a Tibetan Buddhist teacher, Chögyam Trungpa. He's the one who really popularized Buddhism in America. He was friends with the Beat writers and poets, like Allen Ginsberg, and he named the creative writing department at the school after Kerouac, at Ginsberg's suggestion. While I was there, I heard Beat writers speak and took writing workshops with them, but there were also classes in Buddhism and meditation. So I took some of those classes, and that's what really started my devotion to the practice."

I was intrigued. The next night, I said I'd like to join him, and we headed over to the boardwalk right after my shift. We meditated for 20 minutes before I could no longer take it. I got up, he bowed goodbye, and I returned the gesture and walked home.

We kept up that schedule for the next three weeks. Following meditation, I'd go to a meeting in the Grove or in Bradley Beach, then I'd go home and do my chores and hang out with the other guys. I also dropped by the library and picked up the two books Silver had mentioned. I read and reread them both over the next few weeks. They were more interesting than the AA "Big Book" to me. The Big Book is treated like the Bible and it saves lives, but it is a labor to read at times. These, on the other hand, were much more enjoyable.

During this phase of my life, I felt like I was on the right track, on the "AA beam." I was either in meetings, socializing with my housemates, helping Silver, meditating, or reading. It felt like a spiritual convalescence. Little by little, I upped my meditation time. After six weeks, I was sitting for twenty-five minutes, then walking silently in a circle with Silver for five minutes, finishing off with another ten minutes of sitting. I felt like I was really getting somewhere.

CHAPTER 7

We held a monthly speaker meeting at Last House, and one night our guest speakers were from a group in Trenton. Byron introduced the visiting group and welcomed them to our house, "where the debris meets the sea," he added. Their first speaker was a big older guy who called himself "Billy from Philly." He was brimming with energy and exuded charisma, testifying like a heated preacher before his flock. Everything he said was quotable. He said AA was the greatest spiritual movement of the 20th century. He called all the sober AA members living miracles. He said AA was rigorous but rewarding, that you had to work hard or else you'd fail. His best line that night was that he remembered being too scared to die, but that he hadn't really known how to live before he sobered up in AA.

His impassioned speaking inspired me. I wanted to run a tight program. I wanted to help others. And midway through his story, I decided that I wanted him to be my sponsor. I didn't want to take any chances that I'd go back to my old life, and having him in my corner seemed like a great insurance policy.

Billy was followed by an energetic redhead about my age named Claw, short for Claudine. She wore tight jeans, boots, and big hoop earrings, and a lot of make up. She was fun and flirty, talking like one of the guys, but still feminine and cute. I made sure to catch her after the meeting. We hung out on the back porch, chatting and joking for a while. She was from Neptune City, a few miles from Ocean Grove, and was moving back to the area soon. The more we talked, the more I liked her, so I decided to go for it. "Hey, you know, there's a sober dance next month in Belmar. I'll be in phase III by then. How about you pick me up and we grab a pie at Pete and Elda's and then head to the dance together?"

Her lighthearted demeanor immediately changed. "Joppa, it's an unwritten rule in AA that you should have a year of sobriety before dating," she said in earnest. "I don't want to go through the drama you'll be going through in your first year. I also don't want to be your excuse for drinking again. Ever hear of the three Ms? That stands for meetings, meditation, and masturbation. What's your sober date?"

"March 18, 1984."

"Then, you got a date — March 18, 1985," she responded. Talk about delayed gratification!

Just then, Billy came out on the porch and Claw went off looking to bum a cigarette from someone. I thanked Billy for his message, and out of the blue asked if he'd be my sponsor.

"Are you ready to go to any length for your sobriety?" he asked.

"Absolutely!" I answered with determination.

A few more people from the meeting came out to the porch to smoke, so Billy and I went to a small room downstairs by the kitchen to talk. He laid down the law. He told me I had to call him every day, study the Big Book, and write my fourth step inventory ASAP. We would go over the inventory together as my fifth step.

But I hadn't yet formally done the first three steps. I told him this, and started to say, "I thought— " when he aggressively interrupted me. "You're not allowed to think! Look where your best thinking got you!" It was a lot harsher than when Saint told me I had a broken thinker. His eyes bulged as he angrily leaned over me, pointing in my face. "Just shut up and do the work I give you. In return, I'll save your life. Read the Big Book, call me every day, go to meetings, and don't open your mouth until I tell you to!"

I was stunned. Here, I'd just entrusted my well-being to this man, and he completely tore me apart. He expected me to check in about every little thing in my life and follow his commands without question. I'd made a huge mistake choosing him as a sponsor, and I felt my eyes begin to tear up and a big lump in my throat. And then I noticed Saint. He'd been over by the stove in the kitchen, hanging up pots and ladles, a cigarette dangling from his mouth, all the while watching my interaction with Billy. He calmly walked over, snubbing out his Newport on the linoleum with his boot, looked at Billy squarely, and exhaled a big cloud of smoke in his direction as he drew near.

"Visiting time at the zoo is over, Billy," Saint said firmly. "You'll have to continue this conversation another time." Billy was pissed, but he knew who was in charge. He stormed out of the room, and out of the house, along with the rest of the visiting group and Claw.

As soon as Billy left, Saint chuckled. "That's Billy. He usually impresses newcomers, but then he scares them away from AA when he goes off on them. Remember, everything from AA is a suggestion, and the supposedly wise gurus are just drunks themselves."

Saint sat down, continuing, "There all sorts of sponsors, and one man's program could kill another man. Some sponsors are laid back and act like a friend. Some will only work the steps with you and stay out of the rest of your life. Some go real easy on guys and get taken advantage of. And, some are like Billy. Choosing a sponsor and working a program are completely personal, and what you need from a sponsor can change over time. It's all subjective."

I knew for sure I needed a different approach than Billy's. I walked to the pay phone down the street, so I could call him while I knew he was still on the road and couldn't answer. I didn't want to see him, much less talk to him again. I left a message saying I'd changed my mind — thanks anyway. After I hung up, I thought about the approach I'd want to take with a sponsor and the traits I'd want him to have. My mental list of qualities led me to one person: Saint.

When I got back to the house, I found Saint and asked him, "Hey Saint, would you be my sponsor?"

"I'd be honored to."

We stood and looked at each other for a moment, me grinning, Saint dour as usual. Then he cut the silence.

"So, Tony, do you admit that you've been a complete douchebag? That you need to follow the AA program and ask your higher power to lift you out of the shitty mess you call your life?" Saint pointed at me. "This shit's no joke. You better be serious about it, because there are plenty of other guys out there who are and could use my help."

"Damn, Saint," I said. "You don't mince words, do you?"

"Yes or no, Joppa — it's that simple. The right answer might just save your sorry ass."

"Okay, okay — yes! That's why I asked you to sponsor me."

Saint smiled and punched me in the arm, then gave me one of his death-grip handshakes. "Okay then. Welcome to your new life, Joppa. Let's get started."

I followed Saint down to the basement, where he handed me a copy of the Big Book. It was well-worn, unlike my barely used one up in my room. "So, first off, just keep attending meetings, talk about how you're really feeling, and study the Big Book. Don't read it straight through, like a novel — study it. It'll show you how absolute fuck-ups — guys who seem completely doomed — can find sobriety and spirituality."

"Above all," he continued, "keep away from the first drink, then the rest is gravy. You might start to dream big — start looking for a sober girl, try to help others, and even make some money. The things you want may or may not happen, but, always, your sobriety has to come first."

I opened the book, and he told me to start at the Doctor's Opinion. I read it aloud. Then we continued on, reading together and taking frequent pauses to discuss what we'd read and how it applied to us. He even began to reveal bits of his own life and history with AA. I was elated. I felt like I was embarking on an important journey, with someone strong and wise by my side.

Shortly after I began working with Saint, I volunteered to speak at the Sea Bright Monday night meeting, representing my Salvation Army home group. When you agree to a speaking engagement, you travel to another AA group, usually with others from your own group, and you simply tell your story. You have about 20 minutes to talk. There were at least 60 people in the room that night, and I was a little nervous about getting up in front of the crowd. Thankfully, I wasn't going first and had some time to breathe and relax.

The first person to talk was Duncan, a Scottish immigrant who'd graduated from the Salvation Army program a little while before. "I pulled a lot of geographical cures to fix my sorry-ass life," he shared. "I was trying to find the place, or thing, or person that would make me feel fulfilled. But wherever I went, I was the same me, doing the same things, with my actions producing the same results. The same types of people would crop up, I'd make the same mistakes, and I'd still be unhappy. Doing the same thing repeatedly and expecting different results — we all know what that is, right? It's the definition of insanity."

Next up was Mark, an Atlantic City native with a southern Jersey accent. "I seem to only learn from painful lessons," he began. "I work as a realtor now, but before I was sober, I was always changing what I wanted to be: gangster, monk, social activist, rock star, whatever. I was never good enough or part of the crowd, but I still managed to be grandiose. I'd only reminisce about the good times, always leaving out the bad part of the story. My life is so much better now. AA is a simple program — not easy, but simple. After putting the plug in the jug, you just have to change everything about yourself. People call AA a cult — they say I've been brainwashed. But, hell, if I have been brainwashed, obviously my mind needed a good washing anyway!"

And then it was my turn. I made my way up to the front, faced the group, and started my story. "I used to be a regular at Donovan's Reef across the street — a surfer who couldn't surf and a rocker who couldn't play an instrument. I was self-delusional and infantile to the extreme. Thinking about my drinking career, it was all beaches and bars and dreaming about becoming rich and famous. It often felt like I was waiting around for a woman to come into my life or for my real life to begin — the one where I became a big-time dude." I finished out my 20 minutes with anecdotes I thought were funny, AA clichés, and letting go of some truth. I don't know if anybody got anything out of what I said, but I felt like a million bucks when I was through. I was in a "pink cloud" period — a newcomer who'd emerged from an unfulfilling, harmful alcoholic life, to feel happier, healthier, and, for the first time in my life, optimistic. I was content, and I felt more secure than I ever had before.

CHAPTER 8

AA describes alcoholism as a disease of the body, mind, and spirit. Being off drugs and alcohol, and living the AA program, I certainly felt a physical, mental, and spiritual uplift. My long daily walks and some time with weights in our workout room boosted my energy and helped me get in shape physically, and my meditation work with Silver helped exercise and expand my mind. I hoped that with a stronger mind would come better decision-making abilities. Silver had also begun to tutor me in Buddhism, encouraging me to practice mindfulness by staying in the present moment, not dwelling on the past or worrying too much about the future. He'd lent me his copy of *Zen Mind, Beginner's Mind* by Shunryu Suzuki, the Japanese Zen master who started the San Francisco Zen Center. I devoured it.

One day, as we worked together on a project at one of the Fort Hancock army buildings, I brought up something I'd been noticing during meditation. "Hey, you know, sometimes when we're sitting, I hear a quiet swooshing sound amid the silence."

"Kerouac called that the roaring silence of the diamond in *The Dharma Bums*," he replied.

I nodded. I'd been feeling introspective that whole day, and I mentioned offhandedly, "It's weird, but a lot of good stuff has happened to me since I crashed my buddy's car and got busted."

"A car crash changed my life, too," Silver replied. "I was 25 and I'd just finished my undergrad in parks and recreation at Northern Arizona University, after floating around a couple other colleges and changing my major three times. My parents wanted me to get an MBA, which I wasn't at all interested in, but I went with it and was accepted into the program at Emory in Atlanta.

"On my drive to Emory from Jersey, I hit a storm in South Carolina, near Clemson. I had a bright orange Opel mini-Vette. I lost control and suddenly I was skidding sideways down I-85, then I slammed into the back of an 18-wheeler. It was one of those moments where your life passes before your eyes. But I was okay. Not a scratch on me. My car was smashed, though. I got towed into Clemson, and I remember feeling relieved to be alive as we followed the orange-colored paws painted on the road, leading us toward Clemson University.

"It took two weeks to fix my Opel because they had to send out for parts. Man, that was a cool car. Anyway, during those two weeks, I walked around campus, checked out the pubs, and found Hartwell Lake. That's where I met Val, my wife. She was working on a painting of the lake." He paused and smiled at the memory.

"What did you do when the car was ready and you left for Emory?" I asked.

"I never made it to Atlanta," Silver replied. "By the time my car was ready, I was head-over-heels in love with Val. Considering my near-death experience and meeting her, I'd decided that life was too short to pursue things I had no interest in. I stayed there until Thanksgiving break, selling Clemson T-shirts at the Mr. Knickerbocker shop downtown, meditating, hiking, spending time with Val. And then I went back to work as a park ranger. I think, in the end, I made the right choices. And I'm thankful for that car wreck."

In addition to my community service with Silver, I started working again at Skinny Vinnie's, three nights a week. This fulfilled Last House's employment requirement and kept me in touch with the outside world and my old life.

New and Roy were encouraging, and even though they didn't quite get AA, they were open-minded about it. They laughed at the stories I told about Saint, particularly when he had said I had a broken thinker, and his advice that if I thought I had a great idea, I should probably do the opposite of what first came to mind. I started to tell them about Silver one night, and at the mention of his name, Roy's face lit up.

"Silver, that son of a bitch," he said. "He's over at Sandy Hook? We went to school together — I was a grade above him. His family is big into Monmouth

County real estate. They practically own the entire Asbury Park boardwalk. We hung out together all the time in junior high, but we sort of went in different directions in high school. After graduation, I got drafted, and I heard Silver went off to college."

Silver and Roy's friendship was rekindled when they met at Skinny Vinnie's one night. Silver would drive me there for my shift when he and I were done with our work for the day, and whenever he couldn't, Roy would come pick me up. They laughed when they saw each other again for the first time in years. On the surface, the two of them looked like they'd make an unlikely friendship, but they shared similar life philosophies and any differences between them that might have widened with age and distance seemed to melt away.

Roy came to pick me up at the Hook on one of my nights off from Skinny Vinnie's. Silver and I were sitting around a campfire, warming up from a day out in the chilled, foggy air. Roy sat down and joined us, and we settled into a quiet moment where we all stared at the fire, smelling the burning wood, hearing the waves hitting the shore, and smiling. It was just us, living and breathing, and doing nothing at all. Peacefully, we shared this experience for a few moments before we began to chat.

"Joppa's checking out some Kerouac," Silver said to Roy. "I remember when I first read him. It was the summer between freshman and sophomore years at

Long Branch. There was no turning back for me. I got so into his writing, it made me want to be a writer and an adventurer."

Roy nodded enthusiastically. I could see that he was obviously high — he had bloodshot eyes and a goofy grin that only came out when he was on something. "Good shit," he said, raising a can of Coke. "A toast to Jack and Neal! And of course, let's raise our drinks to one of our very own — Allen Ginsberg from Paterson, New Jersey."

"I'd picked up *On the Road* at an old used bookstore in Red Bank," Silver continued. "I was so drawn to the rambling in it, all the adventures in Denver and California. Then I read *The Dharma Bums*, and its focus on Buddhism and appreciation of nature had me hooked."

"Hey Silver," I said. "You're the dharma beach bum!"

He laughed in response, and Roy added, gesturing toward Silver exaggeratedly, "Gary Silver, the Cohen of Koan."

Buddhism was becoming more and more important to me. For the first time in my life, I felt like I was brimming with faith. The Buddha himself demanded no such faith — he instead wanted his followers to question everything, to find out for themselves the truth in what he was telling them. With that in mind, I'd been reading a lot, trying to find that truth.

Suzuki's *Zen Mind, Beginner's Mind* was so simple and inspirational. When I returned it to Silver after only a few days, he looked surprised.

"I expected you to borrow it longer — to read it slowly, savor its wisdom," he said, handing it back to me. "But," he added, smiling, "I see you enjoyed it. What did you think of the concept of the beginner's mind?"

I remembered the passage he was referring to: "The goal of practice is always to keep our beginner's mind. If your mind is empty, it is always ready for anything; it is open to everything."

"It made a lot of sense to me, especially in my place in recovery," I said. "I wish some of the longtime Last House residents could get that. Byron, Vodka John, and Lance have been there forever, but they don't seem to be progressing anymore."

"Right, in the beginner's mind, there are so many possibilities. But in the expert's, there are really very few. So, always try to stay a beginner."

The beginner's mind made me think of the saying "the longest trip is 18 inches — from the head to the heart." Open mind, open heart. That would make a nice meditation mantra.

Silver and I headed out to the beach to pick up trash. As we worked, Silver started to talk more about the fundamentals of Buddhism and its four noble truths.

"The first noble truth is that life is suffering," he said. "This can be physical pain, craving, grief, or even a minor feeling of dissatisfaction or discomfort. The second noble truth says that the origin of suffering is attachment."

"I could apply that to my use of drugs and alcohol," I interjected.

"That's right — attachment applies to desire, passion, the pursuit of wealth, among other things."

I'd just begun to learn about the four noble truths from my readings, and I wanted to know more immediately. I wanted answers, so I could fix myself.

"So, how are you supposed to put desire in check?" I asked.

"That's in the other two noble truths," Silver replied, smiling. "Think about the first two tonight, and I'll tell you about the other two tomorrow. The way to enlightenment is the eightfold path — it's a journey, not an instant fix."

The next day, as promised, Silver told me about the other two noble truths. "So, where the first two noble truths acknowledge suffering and its cause, the second two explain the cessation of suffering," he said. "The third noble truth is the realization that we can be free from suffering, which is referred to as nirvana. The fourth describes the path toward nirvana, known as the eightfold path — kind of a form of self-improvement called the middle way. Basically, it's living life in moderation — so somewhere between being totally hedonistic and totally self-denying."

I felt I could live a life of moderation, now that I had sobriety and tools from AA. I was getting close to the end of my time at Last House, which meant my navy enlistment was just around the corner. I'd been at the house for over two months already, and I was diligently working my way through the AA steps. By the end of May, I was on the fourth step. The basement had become my recovery headquarters, where I did my step work and read the Big Book. I had a desk in my bedroom, and the kitchen table was always available, but I preferred to work in that dank little basement. It inspired me. I imagined myself as a monk in a musty old stone room, honing my spirituality in solitary contemplation.

CHAPTER 9

I hadn't been back to my old apartment since I'd moved to Last House in March. New covered my end of the rent while Jon was figuring out his next move. I realized I needed some things from there, and Silver was kind enough to drive me over on our way to our Asbury meditation. Passing through Sea Bright, just south of Sandy Hook, I saw my old haunts, which I pointed out to Silver.

"The police department is right in between two of your bars, like a block away from them!" he said, laughing. "You regularly hung out there, got smashed, and drove home even though you knew the cops were right there, looking to nab drunk drivers?" He shook his head and smiled.

I told him I spoke there recently, mentioning how Duncan had spoken there before me. Duncan used the AA expression, "Insanity is repeating the same behavior expecting different results."

"Actually, it was Einstein who originally said that," Silver replied. "AA just co-opted it, wisely."

We passed through Monmouth Beach, and within a few minutes, we pulled up to my old apartment. Silver and I walked in the front door and were greeted by Jon, who was in the kitchen. I introduced them, and then glanced around the apartment — that's when I noticed a good-looking blonde sitting on the couch in the living room.

"This is Debbie," Jon said, as she got up to shake our hands. "I'm moving into her place over in Belmar at the end of the month. We met at St. Michael's. Uh, technically Joppa, we're both here with our community service supervisors."

Jon explained that he was doing his community service over at St. Michael's Church, and Debbie runs the community service program there. She approved his service, but she was on vacation the week he started. When she got back, he thought at first that she was another community service worker, and started bullshitting with her.

"When I told him I ran the place and had worked with his probation officer to secure his position there, he was speechless," she said, laughing.

"That was a couple of months ago," Jon said, "and we started going out about a month ago." Apparently, he'd started moving stuff over to her apartment within a couple weeks of dating.

"Yeah, you know what a drunk brings to a second date, right?" Debbie asked. "A moving van!"

Now it was my turn to be speechless. I stared at her for a second, not sure what to think, then she continued, "That's an old AA joke. My parents are members. They go to meetings around Sea Girt and Wall Township."

I relaxed and we all laughed. While Jon, Debbie, and Silver chatted, I went to my room and grabbed the stuff I'd come for, then Silver and I said our goodbyes. I was happy for Jon. What a great woman he'd found himself. But it also felt a little sad, like the official end of an era — no more Joppa and Jon living together. We were both moving on.

The next week, my case quietly went to court. New's lawyer got a plea bargain behind closed doors: the drug charges were dropped due to my upcoming enlistment and compliance with community service and rehab, but I would lose my license for six months. The judge warned me that if anything like this should happen again, I would not be so lucky the second time around.

At that point, I'd been at Last House longer than the 90 days required by the judge, and I'd completed my required community service hours a few weeks before, although I continued volunteering. After my court date, I planned to stay at Last House for about another month, and then in early August, it would be time for my next phase — the navy.

That month went by too quickly. Before I knew it, it was August, and I was packing up my stuff, getting ready to say goodbye. The night before I was to leave Last House and start my enlistment, I stayed up all night with Byron and Saint. I was scared and I told them so. Scared of boot camp, scared of the navy, and generally scared I wouldn't be physically or mentally tough enough.

"Nah, Joppa," Saint said. "It's the same deal as AA — fake it till you make it. I know you can do it."

We sat in silence for a bit, then Saint, followed by Byron, got down on their knees on the basement floor and prayed. I joined them. It was incredibly moving. I felt so much gratitude for my new life, for meeting these men, and for everything they'd given me.

"I can't believe I'm leaving," I said quietly.

"You're going to do great, Joppa," Byron said. "You know, the greatest regrets in life are the chances we don't take. Failures and rejections fade, but not taking chances can haunt you for the rest of your life. You've got a chance to grow even more."

"AA is everywhere, you know," Saint said. "Share in meetings and get a sponsor wherever you end up. Don't shortchange yourself by keeping secrets. And don't keep looking for that flash of enlightenment. Like Bill Wilson said in the Big Book, often the spiritual path is of the 'educational variety,' and that's just as good."

Saint suddenly straightened up, his face tightening into a stern stare. "What's your fifth general order?" he barked at me.

Ah, I knew this one! Saint had told me to memorize the 11 General Orders of a Sentry, that I'd be drilled on it at boot camp. I straightened up, too, and replied, "To quit my post only when properly relieved."

"Good," he said, smiling. "Now, don't start thinking you're normal once you get in with the guys on the boat. There's going to be a lot of drinking. Remember that alcohol was fun at first, Joppa, then fun with problems, and then just problems."

I completed the fourth and fifth steps with Saint over the next couple hours.

In the morning, I gathered up my stuff and said goodbye to the guys at Last House. It was bittersweet, and I admit I choked back tears as I walked down the front porch steps. My mom was waiting for me outside. I'd be leaving my belongings with her while I was at boot camp, all except my books and albums. Those I would be leaving with Jon. My mom drove me over to his apartment and, after a hug, she dropped me off out front so he and I could say goodbye.

Jon and I chatted while I unloaded my stuff in his living room. He told me that he'd gone to the legally mandated three AA meetings at the Belmar club following his court date, but that it just wasn't for him. He didn't think he was an alcoholic, but just needed to work on his attitude. He also told me he was going back to school.

"I applied to Rutgers for their MSW/MBA program. The long-term goal is to start up a new counseling program emphasizing low-income housing assistance with Debbie. I'll mainly handle the business side of things."

"Having to do community service is a funny way to find a career," I said.

"Yeah, and maybe even my future wife," he said with a grin. "I'd thought about social work before, but being a do-gooder seemed so lame."

"Nah, who gives a fuck what some assholes might say?" I said. "I'm really happy for you. Good luck with it."

"Thanks, man. And good luck with the navy." We shook hands and embraced.

After leaving Jon's, I walked for over an hour to Convention Hall, where I saw Silver's truck parked. This would be our last meditation together at the boardwalk. When I turned the corner of the building, I saw him, already in a seated position, eyes closed. I joined him, listening to the waves crashing down below. The sound and the salt spray resonated with me. As I breathed, worries, anxieties, and that steady stream of thoughts momentarily ceased. I remembered feeling hints of that state in the past when I was stoned, but now it was more real. I heard the silent swooshing sound — the silent sound of contentment. After a short meditation, we both opened our eyes and smiled at each other. "Well, it just so happens to be a full moon. You know what that means, Joppa?"

"All the lunatics are out?"

He laughed. "It is also a traditional time for committing to the five precepts of Buddhism. So, repeat each phrase after me."

We slowly recited the five precepts, vows to refrain from killing, taking that which is not given, sexual misconduct, harmful speech, and intoxicants leading to heedlessness.

"Write me when you can, and look me up whenever you're back in town again, okay?" he said. "And remember: In Suzuki Roshi's words, you are perfect the way you are, and there is still room for improvement."

He pulled out his dog-eared copy of *Zen Mind, Beginner's Mind* and handed it to me. I was touched. We then both gave a spontaneous, sort of tongue-in-cheek, sort of serious bow to one another, and I turned to head to the recruiters office, backpack slung over my shoulder. As I walked, I looked at the book in my hand, noticing that Silver had written his name and address on the inside of the front cover. Scribbled beneath that was "Dharma Beach Bum."

SECTION II

NAVY LIFE

CHAPTER 1

My foray into the navy started at the Recruit Training Command an hour north of Chicago in Great Lakes — also known as "Great Mistakes" by the sailors. I was to be there from August through October, and I learned right away that the military was a completely different world than the supportive, protective one I'd had in AA. I could no longer utilize most of the tools I'd been using for day-to-day life — I couldn't phone anyone, go to meetings, or even read the Big Book. Each of us was issued a little green Gideon's Bible, and aside from the Blue Jacket's Manual, that was all we were allowed to read. I had to rely on myself alone, and summon all the serenity and strength I'd gained from AA over the past few months.

The depiction of boot camp you see in the movies, with the yelling, demoralizing, and constant marching, is not sensationalized. I had no privacy, was allowed very little sleep, and spent untold hours ironing my uniform.

The sailors who trained us spat out the word "recruits" when they addressed us like it was a rotten piece of fruit. I wasn't exactly tall —okay, I was short— and that turned out to be a big deal. They'd line us up by height and it became immediately clear that the tall men were groomed to be leaders. They'd be up at the front on marches, and runts like me brought up the rear. When we'd get to an intersection, the two shortest guys were ordered to perform crossing guard duty, leaving them to scramble after the rest of the guys to fall back into line once the rest of group had passed.

I was also singled out for my age. While only five or six years older than most of the other recruits, to guys just out of high school I was practically ancient. They called me "Grandpa" and "Papa Smurf." We all slept in a big room with about thirty bunk beds. I was constantly surrounded by men, yet I had never felt more alone.

A few weeks into basic training, I started receiving letters from friends, and I was so grateful for them. Jon wrote me that he'd gotten into Rutgers and was taking classes three days a week. He also said he and his parents were getting along better than ever. I had to laugh; Jon had resented his dad, never wanted to be like him —even though they'd always been so much alike— and now he was going to his alma mater.

Claw also wrote me. She'd gotten my address from Vodka John when they'd bumped into each other at the Belmar club. She said she'd moved back in with her parents in Neptune City and she was looking into training for a career to get out of waitressing, where drinking on the job and after work with co-workers was too frequent and tempting. She sent me a beautiful leather-bound journal with a note wishing me luck and suggesting I record my feelings and experiences.

Boot camp went by faster than I'd thought it would. I was out by October and off to the Dam Neck base near Virginia Beach for the next step for us naval recruits — the six-week "A" school program.

"A" school was much less torturous and more technical than boot camp. The best part was getting to choose our orders when it was all over. Those with the highest grades in our class got first choice of assignment —if Pearl Harbor was available and they wanted it, it was theirs.

My grades were in the middle, so Pearl Harbor was likely out of reach, but I still had a decent shot at some good orders, especially on the non-glamorous amphibious ships that Saint had mentioned as easy duty to fill up my enlistment. "If you go for a fancy carrier or something like a cruiser or destroyer, you'll get sent on lots of missions and have lots of brass watching you and making you miserable," he'd told me. "You're not going for a career, so just do your time on an old rust bucket and get out."

Japan was on my list of possible orders. That seemed cool, and I liked the idea of getting to visit an authentic Zen center. But, Saint had warned me that after being busted I needed to be ready to hear a lot of *no*s, and this was one of them. When I asked the instructor if my background check had landed me on the list of sailors prohibited from such orders overseas, he nodded yes. "Sorry, Seaman Joppa."

So, I couldn't go to Japan.

My other choices included orders onboard a tiny frigate in Bremerton, outside of Seattle, or a landing platform dock in San Diego.

I went with San Diego. LPDs could land helicopters on the deck and flood a well deck compartment in order to float out a squadron of assault amphibious vehicles. It sounded interesting, but for the most part, I'd just be carting marines around. Not a lot of glory, but it was regular navy, and I'd joined to save my ass, not to be a hero. I was to report to duty December 23, aboard the *USS Duluth - LPD 6*.

CHAPTER 2

With just a couple weeks to go before my orders, I was able to go home for a short visit. The plan was to either take the train or the bus to San Diego. I stayed with my mom for the few days I was home, and she told me she'd decided to put the house on the market and buy a condo in Hoboken. She'd always been a city girl, and Hoboken was much closer to Manhattan; it was just across the Hudson River. I was shocked, but also happy for her. So much was changing.

Because I was only going to be in town a few days, New decided to throw me a welcome back/bon voyage party at Skinny Vinnie's, inviting people from all the different areas of my life. He hung a big sign on the front door saying Skinny Vinnie's was closed for a private party, and my family and friends took over the restaurant, filling the dining room with laughter and shouts over Roy's acoustic guitar.

The crowd was an assorted mix of older members from my Italian family, neighbors from Colts Neck, buddies from school, old coworkers, and AAs. I loved it. It was fascinating to see these people, who only had me in common, mingling and talking like old friends — my mom chatting with Saint, Byron bullshitting with an uncle, Roy and Saint talking about Vietnam, Silver and his wife laughing with Jon and Debbie. I was warmed by the fact that all the people at Skinny

Vinnie's that night had a little piece of me in them, and there was a little bit of them in me. We shared something.

Jon's family showed up to the party, and his dad seemed more relaxed than he used to be, or maybe he was always like that, and it was just my and Jon's attitudes and youth that made him seem uptight. I overheard a snippet of conversation between my mom and Jon's, my mom saying how thankful she was, Jon's mom nodding with a relieved look on her face. I assumed they were talking about us and the better direction we seemed to be headed in. I got to talk with Jon's girlfriend, Debbie, and found that in addition to being funny, she was a great listener. She told me that Jon talked about me all the time and was really proud of our friendship. I told her I agreed.

I was able to chat for a bit with my old Last House buddies. Saint and I talked about the navy, and I told him how training had gone. We also talked about AA and how I could keep the program in my life while at sea. Byron told me that the house next door to Last House, the one that separated it from the beach, had been torn down, and condos were going up in its place. So, for the time being, Last House truly was the last house on the block. Vodka John gave me a bit of gossip about Claw. He said she was training to become a truck driver, and that she'd put on quite a bit of weight. "She's still cute," he said, "but twice the size she was when you met her." I couldn't imagine that, but I could conjure up an image of her driving an 18-wheeler along

I-95, chomping on a wad of gum, chatting on her CB. That totally suited her.

My navy recruiter, Stallworth, even showed up to the party, but now he was a chief petty officer. "When you're at the ship, don't think of it as just doing your time," he told me, the opposite of Saint's advice. "You should plan on doing twenty years, then retire in your mid-forties and start collecting your retirement pay. Then you can go out and get a job in another field, all the while collecting your military pension. When you eventually retire from that job, you'll be collecting two pensions and social security." I pondered that for a moment and thanked him for the advice, tucking away that bit of knowledge for later consideration.

The party started to wrap up, and I stuck around to help New and Roy clean up. Once everyone had gone, New said he had a surprise and led me out to the parking lot.

"Well, what do you think?" he asked. There in the back lot was Jon's Blue Rose, beautifully restored by Roy and some of his biker buddies. New had funded the effort. "She's a beauty. I couldn't let her waste away. Just look at her now," he said.

The Blue Rose gleamed, looking brand new and classic at the same time. "She's gorgeous," I said.

New and I went back into the office, where Roy and Jon were sitting and talking. We sat down with them, and then we all looked at each other and laughed. It was like déjà vu: Jon, Roy, Uncle New, and me, all sitting in the same seats as the night New bailed us out after our bust. So much had happened in the past nine months. Even though everything felt so familiar, this part of my life, even this part of the country, was already beginning to feel like history to me.

"So," Roy said. "We have an interesting idea for you to think about."

"Okay..." I said, not knowing what to expect next.

They all started talking over each other, excited about their idea. I couldn't quite make it out, but it seemed they had a plan for my cross-country trip. Finally, New quieted the other guys and gestured for Jon to speak.

"I want you to take the Blue Rose to Las Vegas on your way to San Diego, and drop her off at a car collector there. I'm going to need a better car for my commute to Rutgers, and I still have fines and legal fees to pay off, so I'm going to sell her. I got a really good offer from this guy. I was hoping you could give her a final send off."

"And I'm going to come with you," Roy added. "Well, part of the way. I want to check out Memphis and Nashville, and then I'll fly home from there."

I loved the idea. After I dropped off the Blue Rose, I could take the train the rest of the way to San Diego. And I couldn't think of anyone better to go on a road trip with — Roy was not only a good friend, but a veteran of the road and a hell of a mechanic.

The next day was the day my driver's license suspension ended, and Roy drove me to the DMV in Eatontown to get it restored. Afterward, we took a ride up to the Hook to see Silver. I was glad I got to see him one more time before leaving. We decided the best place to chat would be in his truck, where I could drive us around the big parking lot, learning how to handle a stick shift before the road trip started the next day.

CHAPTER 3

We started out early, heading the Blue Rose away from Jersey and past the Eastern Seaboard. Roy took the first driving shift, and after a while we stopped for coffee, then had a late lunch at a diner somewhere near Roanoke, Virginia. At Roy's insistence, I got the chicken-fried steak. The thin, breaded steak, smothered in thick white gravy, blanketed a mound of mashed potatoes and a pile of green beans. I'd never had it before, and I've got to say, that was good stuff. We had an older flirt of a waitress who couldn't leave Roy alone. "I just love bikers, even Yankee bikers," she purred to him in her Southern accent as she poured our coffee. Roy beamed as she turned to check on her other tables, swinging her hips as she walked away.

We got back in the car, and it was my turn to drive. Time flew by, and suddenly we were crossing into Tennessee. We saw a Starvin' Marvin gas station, and we liked the name, so we stopped for gas, more coffee, a piss break, and some snacks. As I pumped the gas and Roy washed the windshield, he told me about his time in the South doing training during Vietnam. "I learned a lot about Southern culture living down here and serving alongside these Southern boys. You probably learn more about people from observing them than you do from interacting with them."

We went inside to pay and Roy bought me some marshmallowy, sugary cookie thing called a Moon Pie. Taking our money was a young, lanky country boy with a crew cut. He grinned at us Yankees and drawled, "Combine that with an RC Cola, and you have what's known as the working man's lunch."

Roy and I hopped back in the Blue Rose and headed back down the highway. The Nashville skyline appeared on the horizon just as the sun was going down, and we planned to find a motel for the night. It had taken us thirteen or fourteen hours to get there from Jersey. We got off at the Broadway exit, where the Country Music Hall of Fame was, figuring that would be in the middle of all the action.

Surprisingly, there were adult-oriented businesses in the historic Lower Broadway district. Gentrification was still new in the area, so the neighborhood was a mix of new higher-end bars and shops, with strip clubs and dive bars squeezed in between. After a few blocks, we came upon the Ernest Tubb Record Shop. Across from that was a rib joint with an adjoining country music bar. Roy started thumbing through old country, rockabilly, and blues records at Tubb's while I walked across the street to order ribs for us. We might have arrived after the neighborhood's original heyday, but its spirit was still alive and well.

I got us a table, and while I waited for our food, I scanned the place. Near the door to the bar was a table with four or five rowdy guys in their thirties. The rest of the place was quiet. When the waitress came around to bring the food to our table, the rowdy guys got up and went over to the bar next door. It turned they were the band that was going on next. Moments later, Roy pushed through the swinging doors of the restaurant, looking like a triumphant cowboy in a Western movie. Except instead of a pistol at his side, he had a stack of records under his arm.

We ate our food and watched the band set up next door. Roy was commenting to me on their instruments, and when he finished his last rib, and licked his fingers, he got up and started chatting with the band. They were talking blues and '60s music, having a good time, when Roy pulled his harmonica out of his jean jacket pocket and played a couple riffs. They loved it and invited us to their show, with the promise that Roy could come up and jam with them.

We drifted over to the bar next door and got a table near the stage. Their first set was a mix of '60s pop and R&B songs done with a country twang, plus some well-known country classics. Roy tapped along to the music and chugged Budweiser long necks. I nursed seltzers with lime as I checked out all the southern gals drinking and dancing.

At the start of the second set, Don, the bandleader, motioned for Roy to join them. The band played the intro to Johnny Cash's "Folsom Prison Blues," with its bass-dominated freight train sound, as Roy approached the stage. Don grinned and explained,

"We got an express train from New York City that just arrived. Onboard was this here outlaw harp player. His name is Roy, and he plays harmonica for a New Jersey band called the Twitchin' Chickens. He's all right, despite being a Yankee from hell. Let's give him a big hand everybody."

The crowd hooted and hollered as Roy wailed on his harmonica. They couldn't get enough of him. Twice, at the end of a song, Roy nodded thanks and started to head off the stage, but the band kept waving at him to stay on. He ended up playing the whole second set with them, and they threw in some more blues, a James Brown medley, and a couple Bo Diddley classics to let the harmonica shine.

Roy played with such energy and intensity, like a man on a mission to prove himself beyond the confines of the Jersey Shore. The band, and Roy, closed with a thundering version of "Orange Blossom Special." Roy blew on that harp so hard his face was red and dripping with sweat. When it was all over, the crowd clapped wildly and Roy and the boys looked exhausted but totally happy. They came off the stage and downed some cold beers, celebrating. It was a spectacular show, but honestly, I'd had enough of the bar scene and was ready to head back to our room at the Motel 6 down the street. I told Roy I'd meet him there, and when I turned as I left, I saw the bassist handing Roy a shot of whiskey. This was Roy's night.

Early the next morning, some kids in the room above us were jumping and running around and yelling. I was already awake, but their commotion was a bit early for hungover Roy. He grumbled as he got up out of bed, and slowly got dressed and packed up his stuff. We figured we'd seen the best of Nashville the night before, so now it was time to hit the road toward Memphis, which was about three hours away. Roy's flight back to Newark was at 10 am the next morning, so we only had today to get in all the sites we wanted to see — Graceland, Sun Studios, and Beale Street.

I was at the wheel that morning, moving forward with the road — and with my life — while one of my heroes was slumped over in the passenger side trying to get right. Roy had bought some Goody's powder at the gas station convenience store, which was basically crushed aspirin, and he slid it straight to the back of his throat with a piece of the wax paper wrapper. An hour into our drive, we stopped at the next Waffle House we came across along the interstate. We slogged through the massive pile of food on our plates in silence. We both had steak and eggs, washed them down with ice water, and just about emptied the thermos pot of coffee on the table. Soon enough, we were back on the highway, driving through miles of green countryside that all looked the same to me. I continued at the wheel, and Roy napped for a bit.

When we pulled into Memphis, Roy finally came back around to his usual self. The first stop on our sightseeing tour was Sun Records Studio, where

Elvis, Johnny Cash, Carl Perkins, and other blues and rockabilly legends got their start. After the tour, Roy practically bought out the gift shop, and then we headed to Graceland, where, again, Roy went crazy buying souvenirs. I liked Elvis as much as the next guy, but his house was so gaudy. It was a weird place, making for a weird tour, but I'll admit that Roy and I both teared up a bit when we got to his grave at the end.

It was late afternoon by that time, so we made our way down to Beale Street. We walked around for a bit, and then ducked into a hole-in-the wall advertising a fish fry and live music. As we ate a delicious dinner, an acoustic guitarist played the blues. Afterward, Roy felt like a beer, and we both wanted to hear more music, so we wandered into blues bars up and down Beale Street for the next couple of hours. By 8 o'clock, we were both beat and decided to head back to the motel. I didn't say anything, but I was glad to call it an early night because I wanted some time in the room to just hang out and bullshit with Roy, just the two of us with no distractions, before we went our separate ways the next morning. I think he probably felt the same.

At the airport in the morning, it was hard for me and Roy to say goodbye. We struggled with words, and ended up just shaking hands, then giving each other a side hug. Roy handed me a mix tape he'd made for me for the rest of my trip, said goodbye, and turned to walk into the terminal.

I drove away, totally alone for the first time in a long time. It didn't feel good.

For a while, I didn't even have the radio on; I was just alone with my thoughts and a big lump in my throat threatening to erupt into sobs. As AAs often say, "When alcoholics find themselves alone in their own head, they are in a bad neighborhood."

My thoughts strayed to extremes, and they kept coming back to the brothels in Nevada that I'd heard about. I knew that visiting them would be a bad idea, but I kept thinking about them. I needed some distraction, so I turned on the radio and tried to enjoy the music without letting my mind wander. I prayed to God to help me not do anything stupid. Then I remembered Roy's tape, so I popped it into the cassette player, and the first song was Rick Nelson's mellow "Garden Party."

"Weird choice," I thought.

When the song ended, Roy's voice came on. He'd recorded me a message.

"No, I didn't include that song just because it mentions Chuck Berry, Dylan, or John and Yoko," he said. "I wanted you to hear the line 'you can't please everyone, so you've got to please yourself.' You've got a fresh start. Don't worry about impressing me, your uncle, or Jon. Be your own man, Joppa. In the navy, you can reinvent yourself. We're all rooting for you. Believe me, you will be missed, buddy."

Damn. I was deeply moved by Roy's message and his encouragement. The rest of the tape was more typical of Roy —a mix of blues classics, novelty songs, and Roy playing solo and with the Twitchin' Chickens. I no longer felt so alone.

With no plan for stops or sightseeing, I just kept driving. I listened to Roy's tape three more times before switching back to the radio.

I had plenty of time to think, not think, stare at the desert scenery, and watch the world fly by. I drove until I was exhausted —18 hours— almost to Albuquerque. I got a motel, flopped down on the bed still wearing my clothes, and instantly fell asleep.

CHAPTER 4

When I woke up the next morning, I knew I needed a meeting. My spirit needed rejuvenation after that long, lonely drive. I'd also heard there were a lot of New Age-y people living around Santa Fe and Sedona, so I wanted to see if I could find any Zen centers. Santa Fe was just over an hour away, so I decided to head there and maybe spend a couple days, since I had the time. As I drove, I couldn't believe the New Mexico landscape. It felt mystical — so colorful, with otherworldly land formations and bizarre-looking plants. Once I reached Santa Fe, I was fascinated with its uniquely Southwestern architecture, flat rooftops, and earth-tone adobe. I explored the historic downtown and checked out the galleries of Southwestern art and old pueblo-like buildings. It felt like I'd wandered into a cowboy movie.

While I was downtown, I found a pay phone and looked up the local AA hotline. A meeting was starting in a few minutes, right down the street. There were around twelve people there, and I shared everything that was going on with me: my road trip, my loneliness, wanting to revive my Buddhist connection, the Blue Rose dropoff in Vegas, and my trepidation about this next phase in the navy. It felt so good to get that all out and clear my mind a bit.

Afterward, I joined most of the group at a Mexican café, where we sat out on the patio enjoying tacos and getting to know each other. They were a laid-back group, mostly older hippie dropouts. I was sitting next to the youngest person in the group, a guy named Billy. He was wearing a big straw cowboy hat, paint-splattered tank top, and baggy carpenter pants. He was tanned and muscular in a lean, wiry way, and, like me, he was on the short side.

As we divvied up the check and got ready to leave, Billy asked if I needed a place to stay. "I live at a Zen center that's under construction. If you can help out with some digging, I can give you dinner, a place to sleep, and access to a meditation hall." I couldn't tell if he was joking, and the skepticism must have been apparent on my face, because he added, "No, seriously."

"Yeah, that would be great, thanks!" I said.

After saying our goodbyes to the rest of the group, Billy and I headed away from the Santa Fe Plaza, walking two miles up a narrow, twisting country road until we reached the Zen center, a compound of adobe buildings nestled in a sparse canyon surrounded by snowy mountains.

"It should be open to the public by next year," Billy explained. "We just have to finish landscaping, painting, and a few other details. I have a small crew of college kids living here who help out for their room and board."

As we walked by a line of newly planted trees, Billy bent down and adjusted a sprinkler. "I've been sober over a year now, but before I came here, sprinklers used to be my wake-up call and shower. I was living in a park in Taos, about a mile from where my wife and kids lived. I'd go visit them once a month or so, but I was essentially homeless."

We entered the meditation hall, and it was beautifully decorated with wood paneling and Buddhist statues. Billy explained that he and the crew ate meals together and sat for meditation at sunrise and after dinner. We walked through the hall and out the other side, where the crew was working on planting fruit trees and bamboo. Billy grabbed two shovels, handing me one, and said, "Let's get to work." For the rest of the afternoon, I helped with the landscaping, and one of the college students and I moved some statues behind the main building. Then it was time for dinner.

We gathered in the dining hall and shared a family-style vegetarian dinner, then made our way to the meditation hall. Our meditation cycle included a half-hour of sitting, followed by a five-minute walking meditation, which we repeated once. I hadn't meditated with others in some time, and I found their presence to be a great influence on my ability to stay with it the whole time. After meditation, Billy showed me to my simple room, and I drifted off to sleep feeling content and happy to be there.

In the morning, we sat for meditation, then had breakfast. As I got up after our meal, expecting to help more with landscaping, Billy motioned toward me, and I followed him out to his truck. "I want to take you to Ojo Caliente, a hot springs spa about an hour from here," he said, handing me a pair of swim trunks. "Technically, it's official Zen center business. We need to pick up landscaping stones from a place near Taos." That sounded great to me, so I hopped in the truck and, after gassing up, we headed out.

The hot springs were amazing. They consisted of a complex of baths, each containing different minerals, plus a cold-water pool. For three hours, we went from pool to pool, occasionally dipping into the cold pool and lounging in beach chairs, with the breathtaking multicolored desert canyon walls as our backdrop. It was exactly what I needed after all that driving — both physically and mentally relaxing. My neck, back, and shoulder muscles, generally in a state of tension, completely melted.

We got back on the road to Taos. The landscape along the way changed, becoming greener and less sparse than it had been near Albuquerque and Santa Fe. Billy said it was the high desert, and the plants I was seeing were sage and juniper. We got to the landscaping shop, loaded up the stones, and then turned around and headed back to the Zen center. It was dinnertime when we got back, and after eating and cleaning up, we sat with the crew for evening meditation, then I headed to my room to pack up and get back on the road.

Billy followed me. "Thanks for all your help. Are you sure you don't want to stay one more night?" he asked.

"Thanks for everything," I said, "but I really have to get on the road. I'm running out of time to get to San Diego." Truth be told, I loved it there. I'd have stayed another month if I could.

CHAPTER 5

I made it to Gallup, New Mexico, about three hours from the Zen center, before I felt too tired and stopped for the night. I stayed at a cheap roadside motel, and was up, showered, and back on the road before sunrise the next day. I wasn't exactly excited about the navy, but I was looking forward to California and a new chapter in my life. Daydreams of California beaches had me singing along with the radio. The sun came up, and the miles melted away.

My last major stop before San Diego was going to be Vegas, still hours away. I'd have to pass through Sin City to reach paradise. Thoughts of brothels kept tugging at me. I couldn't stop thinking of picking out a statuesque blonde, or maybe a brunette cowgirl, or a petite redhead. Anyone. I just wanted to fuck, and I was becoming fixated on it, and that did not feel good. My serenity had been disturbed — demolished, really — held captive by these obsessive thoughts. I drove on in discomfort for hours, half the time thinking about hookers and the other half wondering if I should find a pay phone and call Last House for a reality check.

I stopped at the Painted Desert and gazed out at the lonesome, beautiful scenery. The excitement I'd felt earlier had dissolved into nervousness about the future, and near-panic over my obsessive thoughts about brothels. I stood there and breathed, trying to center myself. The sun shone brilliantly, and the silent swooshing sound permeated my being. I was alone — except for a large raven standing on the dusty blacktop nearby, looking bold and dignified. Was he a messenger, a guardian watching over me? I decided that, yes, he was there to keep me company and keep me on my path. It was time to drop the Blue Rose off and get onboard the *USS Duluth*. I got back in the car and headed west.

As I got closer to Vegas, the brothels loomed larger and larger, even though I'd tried to push them out of my head. I'd created this fantasy bordello in my mind, and my thoughts were getting pulled in that direction more and more. I prayed as I drove. At a truck stop a while back, I'd seen an ad for several whorehouses in Pahrump, west of Vegas, and when I neared the exit for Pahrump, I slowed down. I was hesitating. But I was also praying, at first in a whisper, then I was screaming, "God help me!" And He did, or maybe the raven did. I steered toward Las Vegas.

I thought of some dharma wisdom Silver used to paraphrase: "The greatest hero is the one that can conquer himself. This is greater than a warrior that has defeated a thousand men in a thousand battles." I was my own worst enemy, and for that moment, I had conquered myself.

I passed right through Vegas without stopping and headed north to Mount Charleston, where the guy who was going to buy the Blue Rose lived. It was about a 40-minute drive from Vegas, and as the road climbed in elevation, I passed through desert and into mountains. The ever-changing scenery and fresh mountain air lifted my spirits. I saw a yellow caution sign along the road depicting a donkey or horse, and sure enough, a few minutes later, I saw a wild horse way up the hill off the side of the road. Perhaps this was my next guardian, after the desert raven — a stallion running free high up in the clouds.

The wilderness gave way to civilization, as log cabins began dotting the pines. I soon came to the car buyer's address, and turned into a driveway that ended at a ski chalet–style log cabin. As I pulled in, I saw that an AA symbol sticker adorned the mailbox. I parked the car and started to get out at the same time the front door of the cabin opened, and I called out, "Hi, I've got a classic car for a friend of Bill W.!"

"Oh, so you're a friend of Bill's, too?" he replied. "Well, I'm Darwin Scott, and it's nice to meet you." Darwin was a body builder and B-movie actor, which was apparent immediately just based on how he looked. He was probably the best-looking guy I'd ever met. He smiled as he shook my hand — all bright-white teeth —and I saw his face brighten as he looked behind me at the Blue Rose. He walked around the car, silently admiring her for a moment, before saying, "Hey, let's take her for a spin."

"The keys are in the ignition," I replied.

After the test drive, it was a done deal. Darwin loved the Blue Rose as much as Jon and I had. We signed paperwork and exchanged money in his living room, and then he invited me to have a cup of coffee with him. We sat on his rooftop porch overlooking the piney canyon below, and he told me about his journey toward sobriety. He'd been trying to get sober for almost twenty years, and was close to nine months at that time. His relative celebrity made it hard for him to find anonymity and privacy at meetings, and his wealth made some of the consequences from alcoholism less devastating.

"I go to a few privately held meetings each week at the homes of other AA members who have a similar situation as me," he said. "It just feels more comfortable. I know the people there aren't going to try to suck up to me, or con me, or tell all their friends that Darwin Scott was at the meeting that night. And I hold a meeting at my place every week, too, right in my backyard. It's tonight, if you want to stick around for it." Of course I did.

As we chatted, the mailman drove up, got out of his van, and walked over to Darwin's mailbox. He was an older black man with glasses, and he looked vaguely familiar, but I couldn't place him — how would I know a mailman outside of Vegas, anyway? He stopped to say hello to Darwin, then looked at me and paused.

"Excuse me," he said to me. "You from Jersey?"

Holy shit. It was Corners, the disheveled drunk from Asbury who disappeared from our Salvation Army meetings, the one with the "pussy beads." I didn't recognize him all cleaned up, but I certainly recognized his voice.

"Corners?" I said. He nodded, smiling. "Wow! You look like you're doing well. I'm happy for you!"

"Hey man, they've got great meetings in this town," he said. "I'm coming up on six months of sobriety. I'll be back here later for the meeting tonight and we'll catch up then." He got in his van to continue his route.

I couldn't believe it. I'd never seen such a quick — and complete — transformation. Of all the guys I met in Asbury, he was the one I least expected to sober up. I never even thought I'd see him alive again. Darwin told me that Corners lived with family in North Las Vegas and that he'd sometimes come to the private meetings at his house. Corners, who I also learned was really named Cornelius, got sober through the VA and then got his job with the post office. Instead of being called "Corners," here they called him "Cornelius the mailman." I loved it. I couldn't wait to tell the boys back in Ocean Grove.

After Corners left, I helped Darwin set up chairs outside and get a campfire going for the meeting. While he brewed an urn of coffee, I put up a sign in front of his mailbox that read, "WAY OUT AA MEETING" and had a cartoon drawing of an alien wearing sunglasses with an AA symbol on its chest, a nod to nearby Area 51.

Darwin expected about 25 people to show up, and he reminded me that those coming were well-known in the community and highly valued their privacy. The attendees started to show up, and there ended up being an assortment of lounge singers, musicians, magicians, comedians, clowns, gangsters, showgirls, impressionists, acrobats, and an Elvis impersonator. And, of course, Corners. He and I caught up for a few minutes before the meeting started, which was good because he had to leave before the meeting ended.

The meeting itself was ordinary, although it was filled with extraordinary people. As it went on, we threw sticks into the fire as representations of old resentments we sought to let go of. I dug my fourth step out of my sea bag and chucked it into the fire. I felt a little lighter as it transformed into ashes.

After an hour, people started to leave, until it was just me, Darwin, and Doug, the Elvis impersonator. It was late at that point, and Darwin told us, "You're both welcome to stay, but I'm hitting the sack."

"I have my sleeping bag in my truck," Doug said. "I'd love to just camp out here under the stars, if you don't mind." That sounded great to me, and Darwin said he had a sleeping bag I could use and extra bedding, so we went inside the house, grabbed what we needed, and said goodnight to Darwin, settling ourselves outside by the campfire.

Doug wasn't much older than me. He'd come out to Vegas from Steubenville, Ohio, ten years earlier. His older stepbrothers worked in the casinos and he thought he'd give that a try, too, but then the Elvis gig came along. We chatted a while, and then I brought up the brothel obsession that had dogged me on my drive. Doug laughed.

"I feel you," he said. "It's hard to resist. I've been to those places a few times. You didn't miss much. It's simultaneously a thrill and totally mortifying. You have to ring a buzzer to get in, and you're greeted with a line of average-looking chicks, mainly white girls with an Asian thrown in, along with the madam. The madam asks if you want any of them right off the bat, which is awkward, because usually you don't. So, you say no and then go hang out at a cowboy bar with a few other guys, where the hookers are mingling with the patrons. A girl will approach you as if you're at a regular bar and she's being friendly, which feels weird, because you both know that's not what's really going on. You chat for a while, and then she asks if you want to party, which actually is a request to go to her room and pay for sex. You can go with her or hold out for another one more to your liking. When you do get one you want and go to her room with her, you just negotiate for a bit, then pay her, then fuck her. Honestly, it's weird and embarrassing."

"Okay," I said. "I think I made the right choice."

As we settled into our sleeping bags, Doug told me that the train to LA left at 1 pm and he offered to give me a ride to the station, suggesting we get breakfast first, and stop at his place on the way, where we could both clean up and he could grab his gear for his 2 pm performance. From LA, I'd catch another train to San Diego, and I'd arrive with a few days to spare before I was to report for duty.

At the train station the next day, Doug gave me his card and told me to call him anytime. We shook hands, and I grabbed my sea bag and made my way to the station, where I got a one-way ticket. Onboard, I searched for a spot where there weren't a lot of people sitting, so it would be quiet enough for a nap. I could see there was just one person sitting in the back of the car, so I made my way in that direction. As I got closer, I could see that it was an attractive Mexican woman about my age. She was sitting in an aisle seat. I decided to take a chance, and asked if the window seat next to her was taken. She smiled and said no, so I took a seat, and after settling in, began chatting with her. Her name was Daisy and she said she was heading to LA to visit family. She spoke in a heavily accented, but soft, sexy voice. We chatted for a while as the train got up to speed, headed toward California.

Her perfume was as alluring as her full, red lips. She held my gaze and smiled as we made small talk, and I thought for sure she was flirting with me. Was

God rewarding me for resisting the brothels? As a conductor walked by, Daisy asked politely for a blanket, which she then placed over both of us. She leaned in closer to me, snuggling up under the blanket, and then, wordlessly, began caressing my crotch. God *was* rewarding me! She unzipped me and slowly caressed my balls, then she softly ran her long nails along my hard shaft. I turned and kissed her, then felt her body under the blanket — it was supple and firm. I moved my hand up her thigh, up her skirt, and felt how wet she was. She squirmed with pleasure, coming after just a few minutes.

A few moments later, the conductor announced the next stop, and passengers further down the car started collecting their bags and heading down to the doors in preparation to get off. Daisy used that commotion as an opportunity to duck under the blanket and blow me. Just as I was about to come, an old man passed us in the aisle. I don't know if he saw what was happening, but I didn't care — I just closed my eyes and let go. We spent the rest of the ride sleepily cuddled close together under the blanket.

When we reached LA, Daisy planted a wet kiss on my mouth and we went our separate ways. I caught my connecting train, feeling conflicted about what had just happened. I was lonely, but I also had misgivings about meaningless sex and false intimacy. I was going to have to get used to that feeling of loneliness, though, and find a way to deal with it, because soon I'd be on a ship and who knew how long it would be before I feel another woman's body against mine.

The train ride from LA to San Diego was just under three hours. I was required to report to the ship in dress blues, so about midway through the trip, I unpacked my wool uniform and headed to the bathroom to change. The uniform was wrinkled, but there was nothing I could do about that now. As I put it on, buttoning those thirteen buttons below the waist and pulling my pre-tied neckerchief over my head, I examined myself in the bathroom mirror. I looked the part all right, and within hours, I'd be on the ship, assigned a rack and a locker — my new home, a big, ugly, floating gray metal hulk, parked at pier 5, Naval Base San Diego, at 32nd Street.

CHAPTER 6

I learned the realities of navy life pretty quickly. You go in expecting high-seas adventure — carousing exotic locations with pretty islanders, seeing the world while serving your country. That might come later, but while you're in port, being a sailor felt more like being a grunt in a shitty job. It was drudgery, morning to night, with so many rules and bullshit orders. If you weren't cleaning the ship, you were just standing around, waiting for something to happen. There were fire drills, and sometimes you had to pull watch duty on deck, where you shouldered a shotgun for four hours at a stretch, but usually nothing was going on, and you just needed to be ready in case something came up or somebody important wanted you to do something — we called this "standing by to standby." It was so boring, and you felt trapped. Plus you didn't even get to wear the cool uniform — you were in dungarees most of the time. What a disappointment to survive boot camp and end up there. We were always reminding each other to remember this if we ever thought of re-enlisting later.

Our quarters were awful — overcrowded, filled with a bunch of stinky guys, no privacy. The bed, or rack, was just a thin mattress wedged into a metal cubby. It sat on a hinged metal door that opened into what could generously be called a dresser about eight inches deep. That and your locker was all the storage space you got, unless you could snag an extra locker. The worst part of the berthing, though, was that the guys you lived with were also the guys you worked with — you could never get away from them!

I developed a coping mechanism where I decided that while I had to be there physically, doing what I was told and following orders, I would completely check out of there spiritually. I would put in my time, but they didn't own my soul.

The good part of being on the ship was its location. San Diego was gorgeous — the bay, the city skyline, the island of Coronado, and the Coronado Bridge we would chug under when leaving port and upon returning. The weather was perfect. I loved it there. All except that ship.

The other guys were all right, but I didn't bond with anyone in particular. Just like in boot camp, I didn't have much in common with these guys — I was a little older, from an affluent area, and sober. They couldn't understand why I wasn't an officer if I had a degree, why I didn't drink, or what I was doing there at all. I was on the ship a few months before I finally went out with some of them. They'd been talking about going into Tijuana and partying for weeks, and I was always reluctant to join them, but that made me seem like even more of an outcast. So one night, seven other sailors and I crammed into Mac's tank of a Volvo wagon and headed to a parking lot near the border just off I-5 where we picked up a taxi for a dollar each that took us the rest of the way to Tijuana.

None of us had ever been to TJ before, and we were practically electric with giddy, nervous energy. We had a million expectations, and at the same time we had no idea what to really expect. We knew we wanted to go balls out — the other guys were going to get wasted, and there should be enough whores for all of us. We knew we might have problems with the Mexican men — we might get in a fight, or get robbed, conned, or pickpocketed. And we also knew that just crossing the border could get us in trouble with the navy if we got caught. But, none of those negatives mattered when we thought about the girls and getting wild.

When we got out of the cab, we were immediately accosted by little kids begging, trying to sell us sticks of gum. Mac gave them each a quarter and we brushed past them. The streets were filled with hustlers and people looking to party. Tijuana was certainly living up to its reputation, and that only made the trip more exciting.

We made a beeline to a strip joint, where Evans ordered up a round of Dos Equis for the boys and a can of coke for me. While we watched the girls on the stage, the girls working offstage mingled among us where we could grope them, and they groped us right back. If you saw someone you liked, you'd call her over, and pretty soon the two of you would make your way to a private booth behind swinging doors. After several rounds of drinks, my buddies started doing just that. Since I wasn't drunk, it took me a little longer to lose my inhibitions, but after a while, I found a girl I liked and motioned her over to our crowded table. She ended up jerking me off under that table, with my sailor buddies sitting right next to me.

After her, different girls kept coming up to me, and as long as I bought them beers and acted like I was eventually going to pay them for sex, they'd be all over me — kissing me, rubbing my crotch, shaking their tits in my face. That place would have killed me a few years back, before I was sober. And if I wasn't careful, I thought, it still could, despite my sobriety.

After a few hours of debauchery, we rounded up our crew and headed back to the ship without incident, with me as the sober driver. I didn't get drunk, and I didn't fuck anyone, but I proved that I could still party and have a good time like the rest of them. I had become one of the guys.

CHAPTER 7

Ship life was hard for me. It's hard for everyone, but I was still relatively new in sobriety, which is a challenge in itself. Temptation was everywhere. Partying is a big part of social life in the navy, and there were constant opportunities for me to drink, plus it was difficult to regularly attend AA meetings.

The *Duluth* would go on deployment every two years. In between deployments, the crew did short trips out to sea, or work-ups, along the California coast that would last anywhere from three days to two weeks, in order to test the ship's equipment and for training purposes. We did those over a period of 18 months, and then the ship would go out for a six-month cruise. I'd joined the crew about seven months into the work-ups. Between being out at sea for days at a time and standing duty while in port, I couldn't always make the same AA meetings each week, and routinely going to the same meetings on the same nights is crucial for getting to know people in AA and building stability.

The meetings in San Diego were definitely different from the ones back home. They were mainly discussion groups. In a way, this was good, because it gave you an opportunity to get to know the people in your meetings better. But I was used to the way we did it in Jersey, where we had many different kinds of groups and meetings for speakers to tell their stories, with usually just two or three people speaking and one person acting as a kind of a master of ceremonies. The vibe in San Diego was totally different. Everybody would clap after someone shared. We didn't do that in Jersey. People were just way more mellow in San Diego. I don't want to say we were tougher back there, but if someone went on a long, whiny share back home, someone else would eventually interrupt them and say, "Get off the cross, we need the wood." Yeah, it was a little harsh, but we all took it in stride. In San Diego, they'd just keep listening and nodding. It got annoying.

I was able to make it to the Saturday noon meeting in Balboa Park pretty frequently. The last time I'd gone to it, I'd talked about the challenges of being sober in the navy. About half the guys there, it seemed, were ex-sailors who'd been kicked out of the navy for drinking or drugging. They nodded in agreement with me. Later, several of them told me that they wished they'd stayed in, and that they regretted not taking advantage of really seeing the world, instead of just seeing the bars in all the places they traveled to.

I made a friend, Chris, at the Balboa Park meeting. We both went to the meetings closest to the base. He was an ex-sailor about my age from Long Island. He spoke like I did — not just with the same accent, but with the same expressions. We liked the same music, and we were both beach bums and avid moviegoers. Neither of us had much free time to hang out, but it was great to finally have a buddy I could relate to. We'd chat before and after meetings, and sometimes catch a movie after the Saturday park meeting.

Chris loved San Diego; he called it his promised land. He'd served onboard the *Mount Vernon* as a machinist's mate, but was kicked out of the navy five years ago for using drugs. He went on a serious bender after that, and that's when he met his future wife, Becky, a pretty Filipina who was a few years older than him. They met at the Trophy Lounge in National City, which was known as a hook-up spot for sailors and Filipinas. Their relationship lasted beyond casual hook-up, and Becky weathered a few years of Chris' drinking, until he got sober two years ago. With his newfound stability, they got married last year, and they seemed genuinely happy together. Even though the navy didn't work out for him, he landed on his feet, made good money working at the shipyards, and found the love of a good woman. Chris was a survivor, and I admired him for that.

I was also able to regularly attend a meeting right on the beach in Pacific Beach. I was really into PB; it reminded me of the boardwalk cruising spots on the Jersey Shore that I'd always loved, except it didn't have a busy tourist season like Jersey — it was hopping all year round.

Pacific Beach was a mecca for surfers, party people, offbeat characters, and other beach types. I found a little spot in northern PB where I liked to hang out before and after meetings. It was just a little patch of grass with benches, surrounded by palm trees, high up on a cliff, overlooking a good surfing beach. You could see the waves, the beach, and the full horizon. If I couldn't get a seat at one of the benches, I'd sit in the grass. It was mesmerizing to watch the sun dip into the ocean at sunset from way up there. I called it "The Spot" — I don't know if it had an actual name.

I'd found a sponsor in San Diego — Oliver. He was a big guy with a handlebar mustache, an old submarine sailor from the Korean War era. I'd met him at several meetings around town. Oliver lived in an RV and was always moving it, therefore showing up at different meeting locations all the time. I was drawn to him because his bearing and background reminded me of Saint. But once I started working with him, I learned that the two of them were very different. Oliver was mainly hands-off, just there to work the steps with me. He wasn't interested in counseling me on other areas of my life, and he didn't reach out much, but he was always willing to talk when I reached out to him.

I'd pepper him with questions, and he'd answer me with brief kernels of wisdom that sometimes seemed like canned answers, but actually had depth to them: "You're right where you're supposed to be," "Wear life as a loose garment," "Happiness is pumping gas in Bakersfield." I didn't feel the same type of bond with him that I'd had with Saint or Byron or any of the other Jersey guys. But he was levelheaded, wise, and, though I couldn't always immediately find him and his roving

RV, he always seemed to pop up right when I needed to see him.

"You're like my guardian angel," I said to him one day, after he seemed to appear at a meeting out of nowhere.

"God works through people," he said. "And, hey, I just happened to be here. Maybe I needed to see you just as much, if not more, than you needed to see me."

CHAPTER 8

I desperately needed a car. It was unbearable having no transportation while living onboard a navy ship. Just traveling up the levels of the ship to get to the brow was a hike. You had to hike down the ladder to the pier, and then it was a mile or so to get off base. Outside the gates is the rough town of National City, where you either had to keep walking or grab a bus. Not having a car made it really difficult for me to get to meetings.

There was a group of car lots by the base in National City known as "the mile of cars." Sailors were warned by their superiors to keep away from them — the dealers were quick to help naïve sailors part with their money, and their cars were known to be junkers. Naturally, I didn't listen. I went right down there and bought a black Nissan Pulsar, a little stick-shift convertible T-top, for $1,200. I'd never had a sports car, and I always wanted one, especially a convertible, and Southern California was definitely the place to have one. While the Pulsar looked cool, it rattled when the engine was on, there were two bullet holes in the hood, the tires were bald, and the body had some rust on it. I learned quickly that it also burned oil. It finally seized up on me two weeks later. Once again, I was stuck with no wheels, and now I was also out $1,200. I was so frustrated. The whole situation was disappointing because I had hoped that with sobriety would come better decision-making skills, and buying that car had been a dumb decision. I knew it was, and I impulsively did it anyway. And it wasn't just that. I'd been so desperate to make extra money to get that car that I'd gone and donated blood. I went through the ordeal of getting off base, taking public transit, walking to the donation center, getting tested, waiting there for three hours, and then all I made was a lousy $28. I felt like a bum. This was a low point for me in my sobriety.

Poor decision-making and lack of good judgment is common among alcoholics, even in sobriety. We can be fine one moment and doing something stupid the next. That's one reason why maintaining relationships with others in the fellowship and bouncing your thoughts off a sponsor are essential to keeping on track. After my car died, I found Oliver at a meeting near the base. He advised me to just accept the situation, instead of letting myself get frustrated. "Remember, acceptance is not the same thing as approval," he said. "And also remember the AA saying: 'Life on life's terms.'"

He was right, but it was still depressing to me. I'd finally tasted some freedom. I had my own car and could get away from the ship beyond where my two legs and the bus could get me, and now I felt trapped again.

I was really kicking myself. I'd been doing the right thing for so long. I understood good fortune and misfortune can randomly occur, that life works on its own terms, but, damn it, I was tired of what felt like bad luck, and feeling trapped and lonely. I needed to use an AA tool to get out of this funk, and the only one I could think of was to say the Serenity Prayer over and over as I walked on base. So, for what seemed like ten minutes, I said to myself over and over, "God grant me the serenity to accept the things I cannot change, the courage to change the things I can, and the wisdom to know the difference." AAs often criticized "Hail Mary" or "foxhole" prayers — only praying to God when you're in trouble. But it was in times like that when I felt closest to God. I prayed for relief. I prayed to have patience and acceptance.

It did bring me some relief, but I still felt pretty bad. Back at the ship, I remembered the metta practice I did a few times with Silver, which involved sending well wishes, or loving-kindness, to yourself, friends, family, strangers, even enemies. I started practicing metta silently to myself: "May I be protected. May I be healthy. May I be happy." Then I thought of my mother, Uncle New, Jon, Roy, Byron, and Saint, I sent them some silent kindness, too: "May you be protected. May you be healthy. May you be happy." Thinking of my loved ones and sincerely wishing them well made me feel calmer. Next, I sent loving-kindness to people I was friendly with, but who weren't necessarily "loved ones," like Oliver, Chris, and Vodka John; then to people whose names I'd forgotten — former classmates, guys from the navy, old neighbors; then to the entire population in general; and finally, to the people who annoyed me most, from my ex-girlfriend

Melissa to Billy from Philly, my chief, Lance, and others; I wished them all well.

When I was done, I truly felt lighter and more relaxed. But this was fleeting. That old "stinking thinking" — how we AAs refer to alcoholic negative thought patterns and self-destruction — returned when I was back on the ship, and I felt down again. Wallowing in self-pity, I gazed at the rack above mine. I thought of nothing as a lump formed in my throat.

I was in sort of a bad place. While I loved San Diego, I hated the navy and I felt no gratitude in my life. I remembered a guy sharing at a meeting in Asbury, one who said, "A grateful alcoholic will not drink." That had always stuck with me and it felt like a warning now. I needed to change my attitude or I would be in trouble.

One bit of good luck that came my way was another car. Chris bought a new Ford Bronco II and sold me his old '78 Chrysler Cordoba for cheap, allowing me to make payments whenever I could. It was a total pimpmobile — big and gold with curvy sides, plush burgundy interior. And it was in good shape.

Not having a car was one of my excuses for not regularly attending meetings. I had that problem solved now, but there were still other things keeping me from meetings. Maybe I was just getting tired of them. I was a transplant, not feeling strong ties to anyone. I also felt less desperate than when I first started in the program, so I felt less open to suggestion. And the work-ups and irregular schedule of navy life didn't make it any easier. It felt like I was slowly slipping away from the fellowship. Oliver noticed, and when I was at his RV one day, he suggested I sponsor new guys and take on a commitment, like be a greeter or make the coffee at meetings.

"Don't be an AA visitor," he told me. "AAs need to live in AA and visit the outside world, not the other way around."

He was right. Because I couldn't always make the same meetings each week, I didn't take on any kind of commitments. I was avoiding the very thing that makes AA members feel comfortable and like they're part of the group, rather than an occasional visitor or onlooker.

"I want you to envision the most joy-filled times you've had at the beach," he continued. I closed my eyes. "They were when you jumped into the water, weren't they?"

He was right again. I could remember back to when I was a little kid with Cousin Dan over at Sandy Hook, when the whole family spent the day on the beach. We'd stay in the water forever, jumping around, bobbing under the waves. The white water swirled overhead before we would emerge into the salty foam. So, okay, point taken. I needed to be more involved with AA, more in the middle of everything. I'd have to be more outgoing, like when I first started attending meetings back in Jersey. And it would be a good way for me to make friends. Chris was really my only friend in San Diego, and our schedules just did not line up well enough for us to hang out much.

After I left Oliver's, I headed to an appointment I'd made with a counselor, Carol Goldstein. I'd picked up her card a few weeks ago at the PB Alano club, and I'd decided a few days later to call and make an appointment. Her office was in Encinitas, an upscale northern San Diego County beach town. She was a soft-spoken older woman with clear blue eyes and long gray hair, and, she told me immediately, she was a longtime AA member. We recognized one another from the 2:30 daily afternoon meeting at the PB clubhouse that I sometimes attended. We spoke for a few moments in her small office and I told her my situation in a nutshell.

Carol suggested we go outside to talk more. Her office was on the grounds of a Hindu-influenced group called the *Self-Realization Fellowship*. Just outside her office were lush gardens of flowers and other tropical plants arranged around pools filled with koi fish. The gardens ended at a cliff overlooking the Pacific. We chatted as we walked, until we got to an isolated bench where we sat down, surrounded by the sound of waves crashing on the beach below, and the smell of ocean salt and exotic flowers.

"You're not having any fun, Tony," she said, interrupting that peaceful moment.

I stammered, and she laughed. "You're bored. No girlfriend, not enough money. A young guy like you needs those things, along with new experiences, to enjoy a fulfilling life."

Now I laughed. She'd hit the nail on the head. She continued, "I don't think you need counseling. I think you need to go out and have some have fun and keep working with your sponsor. Working the steps and helping others will get you back on track. It will all work out. Not in your time, but in God's time."

I thought about that as I drove away from her office. I knew I needed to get more involved in AA, and I also needed to try to meet women. There were personal ads in the *Reader*, and I'd looked at them many times in desperation, but I now decided to finally respond to one. The one I chose promised "beautiful Filipinas interested in serious relationships with those proudly serving in the U.S. Navy." I wrote a quick note to the address listed and dropped it in the mail. A week later, I got a reply. The girl's name was Wendy. She was 20 and staying with relatives living in Chula Vista. She also sent pictures and she was cute — long black hair, pretty face, and a petite but curvaceous body. I wrote her back a few days later. Now I had some hope.

CHAPTER 9

For all the griping I'd done about being in the navy, I was really excited when I was promoted to operations specialist third class petty officer, or OS3. The promotion was sort of automatic, since there was a shortage of sailors in my job, but it still felt good to move up in rank. I stood on deck as our commanding officer Captain Cruz made his speech, then he walked around congratulating all of us new petty officers, slapping backs, punching arms, heartily shaking hands. This was a big deal.

I'd put up with so much shit in the navy so far, I needed more encouragement like this. It had been hard to find my place on the ship and adapt to the strict hierarchies. Some of the chiefs were complete assholes, just cruel for cruelty's sake. Officers were usually aloof, letting the enlisted underlings do their dirty work. You were always told your place, and it was so frustrating to have to defer to someone who outranked you when you were pretty sure you were the better man. But, of course, AAs always feel like we're either better or less than others — we like to say we're egomaniacs with inferiority complexes. It's hard for us to adapt to being a "worker among workers," as they say, or just another Bozo on the bus.

As frustrating as the hierarchies were, I did find the strict rules and boundaries to be helpful for my personal development. There were no gray areas in the navy, no excuses. I knew that my personality was one where if there was a boundary to push or leeway given on a rule, I was going to try to push beyond the limit. The navy was full of guys like me, and the severity of the rules helped keep us in line. Because otherwise, your ass was going to get chewed out, and that was not fun.

I made an effort to get more involved with AA between work-up deployments. I became a regular at a few meetings, talked to more people, and even tried to sponsor a few guys, but none of them stuck with it. Oliver told me that was common and not to take it personally — a lot of people will try to get started with a sponsor, but drop off pretty quickly after a phone call or two. I also started to reveal more of myself to Oliver. I told him something I hadn't told anyone — that I'd smoked weed with some of the guys one night back in October, during "A" school. After I told Oliver, I felt it was important to admit it at meetings. Nobody judged me when I told them, and it actually appeared to make people warm up to me more. Everyone seemed to have a story about marijuana maintenance, pill popping, and other kinds of slips.

After opening up to Oliver, he started to take me under his wing more and got more involved in my life. He started parking his RV more often at the Strand, a narrow strip of land connecting Coronado and Imperial Beach. When we could, we'd get together on weekends for the early bird meeting at the Coronado

AA clubhouse, then spend an hour or so together at a bagel place on Orange Avenue.

We also started working steps six and seven by reading together in the *Twelve Steps and Twelve Traditions* book, also known as the "Twelve and Twelve." This was where I would summon the humility to ask God to remove identified defects of character. Up to this point, the steps concentrated on getting you out of your denial of your alcoholism and problems, and toward recognizing a power other than your own self. The book says this part of the steps "separates the men from the boys." AA becomes less about alcohol intake here, or symptoms, and now completely about spirituality, or root causes and a solution.

CHAPTER 10

I counted my sobriety anniversary as the day after I smoked weed back in October last year, so, as the *Duluth*'s six-month deployment to the Middle East approached, I was celebrating my first year of sobriety. I'd attended meetings the longest and most frequently at the little coffeehouse down the street from the base. It was a ragtag cast of characters, but they'd known me a while at that point and celebrated joyously with me. I also got a token with a birthday cake at the PB 2:30 meeting. Carol, the counselor was there, and she got some laughs from the group when she told the story about our chat in Encinitas a few months ago. At the Coronado meeting, Oliver gave me a token and told the tightknit group how dedicated I was in working steps six and seven with him. Then he told them that I'd be working on my eighth step list during my upcoming deployment.

The deployment loomed over me. We were set to begin our Westpac — short for Western Pacific cruise — in two months. We got a new commanding officer, Captain Miller, who was a total hardass. He was trying to make his way up the ranks to become CO of an aircraft carrier, then on to becoming an admiral. Every time Miller ordered you to do something, you had to respond with "Sir! Yes, sir!" He'd get on your ass even if you said, "Roger that, sir," which was normally acceptable. He worked us like dogs and had no reservations about chewing us out. I was not looking forward to spending six months at sea with him.

I was able to hang out with Chris a bit more before my deployment. He wanted to get me back into surfing, and I was eager to get back in the water. It had been years since I'd last surfed. One Saturday morning, Chris loaded two of his surfboards onto the Cordoba's racks, brought along an extra wetsuit for me, and we took off for Black's Beach in La Jolla, a legendary surf spot. It was unseasonably warm and sunny for mid-October, a beautiful day to drive through La Jolla. It was the prettiest place I'd seen in Southern California yet. The lush, hilly landscape was exactly what I'd always envisioned California would look like.

We parked near UCSD, then started out on a long, strenuous hike that began at the top of an arid bluff and ended at the beach. This was made more difficult with the surfboards and other gear we were carrying. I took my wallet with me because Chris warned me that cars were often broken into there. When we reached the bottom of the trail, I noticed that no one on the beach was wearing clothes. It was a nude beach. I looked over at Chris with wide eyes, and he was laughing his ass off.

It was a struggle to surf again after so many years. I paddled like hell to get out beyond the whitewater, got trounced and thrown about in the process, and barely avoided colliding with surfers coming in off great rides, but I still managed to catch a few decent waves and hang on for a few seconds before wiping out. Those few moments of riding a wave were like a natural high. Here I was, physically jumping into water, not just metaphorically as Oliver had suggested a few months back. I had a blast. After a couple magical hours in the water, we were ready to call it a day, and trudged back up the trail to the car. Except the car was gone.

We looked at each other in silence for a moment. "I guess you weren't joking about thieves here," I said.

He shrugged. "Yeah, easy come, easy go. There's a pay phone down the street. I'll call Becky to pick us up."

As we waited for Becky, Chris told me he didn't expect any money from me for the car. I was relieved, but bummed out that once again, I was out a ride, and I'd left the journal Claw had sent me under the passenger seat. The Cordoba would probably end up at a chop shop in TJ, and my beautiful leather-bound journal would most likely end up in the trash.

CHAPTER 11

And just like that, Westpac was suddenly only a few days away. After the Cordoba had been stolen, I'd picked up a Toyota Corolla for $400 from a signalman taking orders to Guam who didn't want to bother shipping it and needed some extra cash. I took it over to Chris's in Chula Vista for Becky to use while I was gone. They fed me dinner and then Chris drove me back to the ship.

Back onboard, I called folks back home to say goodbye. I felt like I wouldn't be able to talk to them for a long time, like I was an old-time sailor setting off in a tall ship, sailing to lands unknown, risking a fall off the flat earth. But really, it was only a week's trip to reach Hawaii, and I'd be able to call them from there.

I talked to Roy first, and he was really excited for me, though he was disappointed that the *Duluth* wasn't going to stop in the Philippines, where sailors tend to go wild. I told him that Thailand was the party spot now, and he joked that he wanted some sea stories when I got back. I called Uncle New next, and when I told him I was leaving in a few days, he called out, "Anchors aweigh, Admiral!" He'd started calling me "Admiral" after I'd been onboard for a while. When I talked to my mother, she sounded worried, but said six months would go by fast. I told her not to be nervous — it would be an adventure for me. I sort of meant that.

The day we deployed, it felt unreal. We left the pier and went under the Coronado Bridge, just as we always did during our work-ups. But this time, I wasn't in the cold, dark windowless combat information center — the CIC — where operations specialists spend most of their watch time. Instead, I was next door, on the ship's bridge with Captain Miller, the executive officer, and quartermasters. I was recording data about our travel conditions on a board and relaying bits of information back and forth between the two compartments over the sound-powered headsets. This was way more exciting. I could feel the salt spray, smell the ocean, hear the ship splashing through the water, and when I turned around at one point, I saw San Diego fading into the distance.

Underway, our division was split into two watch shifts, port and starboard. Each shift lasted six hours, then you had six hours off — we called it "six on and six off," or "six and six." Your time was your own in those six hours not on watch, and you tried to fit in whatever you could —sleeping, eating, working out, doing laundry, showering, reading, jerking off, listening to music, or shopping at the ship store. Unfortunately, fire drills and other trainings could happen at any time, and it didn't matter if you were off watch and in the bathroom, asleep, getting a haircut — no matter where you were or what you were doing, you had to immediately jump up and participate. When the drill ended, you might only have an hour or so left to finish what you were doing before you had to go back on watch. I was either down in the ship during my off time or working in the CIC during watch, so there were days when I didn't get on deck and hardly saw the sun — I'd start to lose track of time. It was a grueling schedule.

It took us one week to reach Hawaii, and we were there for three days. A new OS2 joined us there, a cocky little bodybuilder named Williams. He'd tried to become a Navy SEAL, but got kicked out during Hell Week at BUD/S. He was assigned to the rack below mine, and we were on the same watch schedule. The guy had such a bad attitude, and you could tell he was embarrassed and bitter about not making it as a SEAL.

Williams aside, Hawaii was more majestic than I'd ever imagined. Lush hillsides, colorful flowers, pristine beaches, and warm water. Paradise! Every day we were there, it rained, but only for a half-hour or so, and then we'd be treated to a big arcing rainbow. I played tourist while we were there, and immediately got a Hawaiian shirt and lei to wear around when we were out on liberty.

After we left Hawaii, we were at sea for weeks. I was grateful for my off hours. I listened to music on my cassette player with headphones, worked out at the gym, and read novels. I'd picked up a dozen or so books at used bookstores before we left on deployment, and I was especially enjoying *Way of the Peaceful Warrior*. I was also making progress on my eighth step list of people I felt I needed to make amends to. Working my AA program was a challenge, with no meetings and limited access to a phone, so I prayed regularly, just like in boot camp.

But being at sea that long was pure hell — monotonous and confining. It was seriously starting to feel like indentured servitude, and it was a daily reminder that I was only there because of the mistakes and poor decisions I'd made. The drudgery of work when we were on watch was bad enough, but getting called in to help out during off hours was almost too much to bear. It was especially disheartening that I was never able to escape from the work environment or from my shipmates while we were underway.

I'd stood watch all night in CIC one night, and fell into my rack completely exhausted. I'd been asleep for maybe 90 minutes when Williams woke me up and said we were needed on a working party moving boxes of food from on deck to the freezers below. Ugh. I was achy and greasy from work, I hadn't had a shower since the day before because there'd been no hot water, and I just felt gross and tired. I rolled out of my rack and put on my dirty dungarees, then went and stood in line with all the sailors ranked E-5 and below. Hundreds of boxes were passed from sailor to sailor, going all the way from the flight deck, through the galley, and down to the storage area below. This took a couple hours, and I was looking forward to getting back to my rack, but it turned out we had another job to do. We were all ordered to go up to the flight deck to help with receiving fuel. Good Lord, I felt helpless. I started counting the remaining months of my navy career as

I worked. My three-year enlistment began August 10, 1984. There were four more months of Westpac. Then I had fourteen more months before I was out. That might as well have been forever.

We finally made it to Singapore after what seemed like an eternity. I couldn't get off the ship fast enough. I went ashore with a group of five other sailors and we shopped and people watched and tried street food. Soliz had been there before, so he served as our tour guide and warned us to watch our behavior because the place was notoriously strict. I was surprised at how diverse Singapore was — I'd never seen such a large mix of different races and nationalities. We checked out the Chinatown area, which I was excited to see had old Buddhist and Hindu temples. The other sailors weren't so interested, though, and we quickly made our way to the Geylang red-light district.

Geylang was on the list of forbidden areas we were given before going out on liberty. I had to laugh at the list — the ship told us to stay away from these areas, yet also essentially gave us a road map right to them!

"It's on the list, but we can still go there," Soliz told us. "You won't get in trouble for being there. You might get questioned and told to leave, but that's it. Just don't do anything stupid and it'll be fine. If you do something stupid and shore patrol from the ship gets involved, you're fucked."

We climbed into a minivan cab that took us across the city. When the cabbie dropped us off, he winked and said, "Have fun, but don't do anything stupid." Good advice. We scoped out the area and stopped at a whorehouse that displayed its selection of women behind a glass window. They were each sitting on a stool wearing a bikini, and each had a numbered identification card hanging around their necks. Mac and Ortiz each picked out a girl and disappeared inside. The rest of us didn't see anything we liked and headed back out onto the street, where, moments later, Williams and Soliz drifted into a bar filled with what I assume were prostitutes.

That left me and Adams. He was an evangelical Christian country boy. I have no idea how he got dragged along on this little trip, but neither of us was interested in dabbling with the girls there. I'd been tempted, yes. But, I didn't have alcohol to push me over the edge like the other guys did. A big part of me wished I was in that last bar Williams and Soliz disappeared into, getting drunk, finding a girl for the night. But, I'd been through too much and worked too hard to backslide. Discipline and levelheadedness would pay off, I told myself.

As Adams and I made our way out of the red-light district, we passed by a few chiefs from the ship making their way in. They didn't acknowledge us, but they also didn't try to hide. Adams had been scoping out tattoo parlors throughout the day. He'd been wanting to get a simple tattoo of a crucifix on his back. Just outside of Geylang, he found one that looked all right and we headed in. As Adams lay on his stomach getting inked, I flipped through a book of tattoo samples. There were some pretty cool ones in there. I started to consider getting one as my souvenir from Singapore, but that thought was interrupted by a whimper. I looked up.

"You all right, buddy?" I asked Adams.

He didn't respond. Tears ran down his face and he looked like he was in agony. I decided against that souvenir.

Adams was moving slowly and tentatively as we walked out of the tattoo parlor, wincing every now and then. We stopped into a drugstore for gel and other supplies that he needed to care for his healing tattoo, then we found a noodle shop and got to know each other a little better over dinner.

All us guys in the division assumed Adams was from some perfect, God-fearing family, but it turned out he had a rough background. He grew up in foster homes around Las Vegas and lived at St. Jude's Ranch in Boulder City, Nevada. "My next stop was going to be Spring Mountain Youth Camp. I kept getting in trouble for running away, so eventually, my probation officer worked it out so that I could join the navy."

I didn't press him on what he'd done to get into that situation. Instead, I told him my story — the car crash, my punishment, AA, and my visit to Mount Charleston. He told me that he was able to stay out of trouble in recent years because of his affiliation with the church. Just like me with AA.

He laughed, and said, "The other guys in our division think we're the two nerds, but I bet we're the only ones with probation officers."

After dinner, we crashed at a cheap hotel downtown, then grabbed breakfast the next morning before going back to the ship, which was scheduled to leave at 1 pm. We got to the shuttle stop by the pier around 10, but no one was there. We looked at each other, knowing that something had gone wrong.

"Where is everybody?" Adams asked, wide-eyed. We tried to remain calm, but we were terrified that we'd somehow missed the ship's movement, and that was a major offense, the equivalent of going AWOL in the army. In short, if the ship was gone when we got to the harbor, we were fucked.

We took a cab to the harbor, and broke out into a run toward the pier. When we got to it, our hearts sank. The *Duluth* was gone, already on its way to the Straits of Malacca, without us.

"Oh shit!"

"What do we do?"

"Hire a boat to take us out there? Swim?"

"We're fucked!"

We heard a noise behind us and turned to find our supply officer walking toward us, all smiles.

"Hey guys, guess you didn't hear that the ship's departure time was moved up three hours."

"No, we didn't!" I said, still freaking out.

"It's okay," he replied. "You're not going to be in trouble. I'm shipping out from here to my new command, so I stood by just in case there were any stragglers. The *Belleau Wood* is leaving in a few hours. I can get you onboard and you can take a helicopter over to the *Duluth*."

It turned out that everybody but me and Adams knew the *Duluth* was pulling out at 10 instead of 1. We boarded the *Belleau Wood*, part of our three-ship Amphibious Ready Group, still in fear that we were in deep trouble. A few hours after getting underway, we were transported by helicopter to the *Duluth*. When we landed on deck, we were greeted by the command master chief. He also assured us that we weren't in trouble. Our chief felt differently, however. He said it embarrassed him to have two of his sailors miss the ship's movement. We should have called to confirm the departure, or gotten there much earlier, or otherwise somehow magically known that the ship was leaving early. While Adams and I were relieved that we weren't in actual trouble, having your chief pissed at you means you're going to be stuck with every shit job imaginable for a while. And we were.

CHAPTER 12

We'd reached the Persian Gulf in early March, stopping first in Jordan, and then Bahrain. Tiny Bahrain was a glitzy, wealthy country filled with tall skyscrapers, so I was surprised to see the locals still dressed in traditional clothing; I guess I was expecting that with money would come western clothes. The men had big beards and wore robes with their heads wrapped in cloth; the women wore burqas with their faces covered. The locals seemed wary of us Americans. I understood — not everyone viewed our country with reverence or envy. Here, we symbolized western decadence and meddled in their affairs from afar.

Adams and I spent the day wandering around Manama going in and out of shops and looking at the architecture. We eventually caught up with the other sailors, and a big group of us went to a striptease show in a hotel bar. It wasn't much of a show —the dancers were pretty Russians, but they were fully clothed and just sort of swayed and made eyes at us. Word was that they were really prostitutes. Williams was drunk and he kept making lewd gestures at one of the girls, and the bouncer started hassling him. Before we could get in trouble, I stepped between them and told the bouncer we were leaving. Adams and I ushered Williams out into the street and we decided it was time to head back to the ship. "Yeah, you don't want to miss the ship this time, do you shipwrecks?" Williams teased us.

On our way back to the *Duluth*, Williams was on the lookout for a massage parlor. "I went to a few in San Diego. Believe me, it's a good time."

"That's a big fat negative, shipmate," Adams replied. Neither of us wanted to go to a massage parlor. Our main objective at that point was getting Williams sobered up and back on ship.

"Hey, how about kebobs and coffee instead?" I suggested. Williams went for it, and after about an hour in a café, we made our way back to the ship, with Williams in much better shape than before.

From Bahrain, the *Duluth* made its way back to Jordan, and we arrived there on my 26th birthday in mid-March. What a different place I was at in my life from two years before, when I was arrested.

The ship had organized a tour for those of us who were interested in checking out the ancient ruins of the city of Petra, which was about a two-hour bus ride from Aqaba, where our ship was docked. We could ride a camel or a donkey, and I opted for a donkey. The camels were too big and mean looking.

The ruins were amazing — I was expecting old freestanding buildings, but they were actually structures with pillars carved into rocky walls. I didn't feel close enough to any of my shipmates to share that it was my birthday.

On our way back home from the Gulf, the *Duluth* crossed the equator. The navy has what is essentially a hazing ritual for when this happens. It's optional, and since I rarely had options onboard, and I thought this was as stupid as a fraternity hazing, I opted out. It was my one chance to assert some authority over myself, however trivial.

From what I've heard, you got woken up, sprayed in the face with water, sailors dressed up like King Neptune and Davy Jones, and in the end, you went from being a pollywog to a shellback. Then you got a certificate to commemorate the occasion. I regret not getting that certificate.

CHAPTER 13

We stopped in Saipan for a few days on the way home. The first day ashore, some of the guys and I hit a few bars and tried our luck with the local women. Our luck wasn't so good. The second day, we went snorkeling near the hotel and saw all kinds of colorful little fish. I took out a kayak alone, paddling around the reef for a while. As I approached the edge of it, a local in another kayak paddled over to me and warned me to stay back, because sharks frequented the area I was entering. I took his advice and paddled back to catch up with the guys. We regrouped and Soliz once again played tour guide for us, showing us remnants from the Battle of Saipan, where the U.S. beat the Japanese in World War II. He pointed just beyond the reefs we'd snorkeled in earlier and said there were tanks in the water left over from the war. I wish I'd seen them earlier while I was kayaking!

On the third day in Saipan, a group of us left the *Duluth* early, and a few blocks into town, I ditched the guys to explore on my own. I was taking a chance doing this — you weren't supposed to travel without a liberty buddy when you were in a location outside of the United States. I was hoping to find an AA meeting — that or a rub-and-tug massage parlor. It'd been a long time since I'd been to a meeting, and beating off to my Filipina pen pal Wendy's pictures just wasn't cutting it anymore. I knew that a meeting would be better for me, but as I looked through a phone book at a pay phone, I found numbers for both Alcoholics Anonymous and a massage parlor. I called both.

There was a meeting starting in about half an hour, and I was promised "a good time" at the massage parlor. Both were nearby, and I couldn't help but look for the "Oriental spa" first. I found it pretty quickly, and when I walked in, it was practically deserted and the one girl working was taken at the moment. I left, irritated at myself for choosing smut over a meeting, but also for not getting what I wanted.

I showed a nearby shopkeeper the scrap of paper with the meeting address on it and asked him, "Do you know where this place is?" He pointed to a building across the street in a little park. I made it right on time. The meeting was small, about nine people, and everyone was American. We went around the room in a circle, each sharing for a few minutes. I talked about the difficulty I was facing without meetings while on deployment, and the loneliness I'd been feeling. When it was over, I felt a lot better and no longer needed a whore. As I walked back toward the marina, I ran into a group of *Duluth* sailors hanging around a bar and I joined up with them. After a while, we walked back to the *Duluth* together. I was ready to get back to my life in San Diego. We were more than halfway done with deployment — it was a matter of counting down the weeks now.

In mid-May, I received a letter from Wendy. She included her address in Chula Vista and sexy pictures of her in short shorts and a tight T-shirt. I wrote her back, telling her I'd be back later this month and that I looked forward to meeting her in person. Maybe I'd finally found the woman I'd been looking for all these years.

Near the end of deployment, we took our advancement exams. I was hoping for a promotion to second class petty officer. A couple weeks after the exams, the *Duluth* was pulling into the yards for maintenance and Westpac was finally over. I got my test results and I made E-5! Chris, Becky, and Oliver came onboard to watch the promotion ceremony. I felt really proud.

Now that I was back in San Diego, I was looking forward to getting back into regular meetings and just getting out more. Having fun, like Carol had said. Chris and Becky invited me over for a barbeque one night, and they suggested that I also invite Wendy for our first date. The night of the barbeque, I got all spiffed up and was excitedly waiting for her at Chris's house, but when she showed up, I was shocked. She'd clearly sent me someone else's pictures. She was older, taller, and plumper than the girl in the photos — she even had completely different facial features. And she was immediately rude. The first thing she said to me was that she thought I'd be taller. I held my tongue about the pictures not matching reality. Next, she criticized

Chris and Becky's neighborhood, asking if her car would be safe parked out front.

Becky pulled Wendy into the bedroom and proceeded to ream her out in Tagalog. Chris and I stayed out on the back patio grilling and exchanging glances as Becky laid into her. Soon, we heard a car door slam, then a car take off. Becky came out onto the patio and said, "Well, you dodged a bullet. What a bitch."

After Westpac, my remaining time in the navy went by so much faster. I understood the drill, and as an E-5, I no longer had to do much grunt work. I made a few buddies and was able to get to meetings more regularly, and Oliver and I made a lot of progress through the steps.

The last year of my enlistment started with a couple of months killing time on a barge while the ship was in the yards for maintenance. Chris worked nearby, so I was able to have lunch with him pretty often. One day over burritos, he gave me some photos Becky had taken when I got my second chevron. I mailed a few home to my mother, New, and Saint. Roy wrote me later that month that they'd blown up one of the pictures of me in my dress whites, smiling and proud, and hung it over the bar at Skinny Vinnie's — right in between a Budweiser lamp with Clydesdales going around in circles and that old mirror of Yankee Stadium.

In the remaining months, guys rotated off the ship and new ones appeared. Before I knew it, my time was short.

Just a few weeks before I was out in August, we started doing work-ups, and I got to work some shifts as watch supervisor. It felt good to finally be in a more significant role, doing work that seemed to actually have an impact on our ship's mission. For a moment, I considered staying in the navy. Maybe I could keep climbing the ranks, retire relatively young, then get that pension Stallworth had mentioned. That thought was in my head for maybe two minutes before I swept it aside. No way was I going to reenlist. I knew I wasn't cut from that mold, and it was time for a new phase in my life. Now, I just needed to figure out what that was going to be.

Section III

Northern California

CHAPTER 1

"Hey Joppa!" I heard Saint's voice over the phone one Tuesday afternoon.

"Saint! What's up?"

"I'm going to be in the Bay Area this weekend. Drive up and meet me there."

"Hell yeah, Saint! What's going on? What are you doing there? Do you have a place for us to stay?"

"Enough with the fucking questions," Saint said with feigned irritation. I could tell he was just as excited as I was. "Look, I'll tell you the details when I see you. Pick me up at the Oakland airport Friday night. I arrive at 7:10 p.m. on Eastern, direct from Newark." Then he hung up.

I'd been out of the navy for two months at that point, staying at Chris and Becky's place in Chula Vista, and trying to figure out what to do next. They were letting me sleep in their screened-in front porch in exchange for a few bucks here and there. I was collecting unemployment after my discharge, so I was getting by okay — for the next six months anyway, before I'd no longer be eligible for it.

Since my discharge, I'd been regularly making meetings, doing AA service work, journaling, meditating, talking to newcomers, and praying my ass off. Basically, keeping my head down, doing the next right thing, and having faith. Oliver assured me that good things would happen if I remained patient, "Trust God, clean house, and help others."

I drove up to the Bay Area Friday morning. It was a long ride, and I spent most of it wondering what Saint was up to. I suspected he had big news for me, but I couldn't begin to guess what it was. I pulled up to the arrivals area at the Oakland airport, and there he was, smiling and waving me over. I was happy as hell to see him. He told me he had an old navy buddy in Oakland, Roland Jeffries, and that the two of them usually got together every few years — it'd been five years since their last reunion, and he'd be meeting up with him tonight.

We checked into the navy hotel at the reserve base in Alameda, only about ten minutes from the airport, then drove to Jack London Square in Oakland to meet Roland at his condo. Roland was standing by his front lobby door when we got there — a tall, striking black man with a shaved head, wearing a "Mills College Dad" T-shirt and pressed khakis.

Saint got out of the car to greet Roland, and Roland called out to him, "Chief Van Sant. Haven't seen you in way too long!" Huh, I thought, so maybe "Saint" is a play on his last name? They shook hands and hugged, as Saint said, "Not since the funeral. It's been too long."

Originally, we'd planned to drive into San Francisco for dinner, but Roland started talking up a local barbeque joint so much, we decided to stick in Oakland and put in a delivery order from there instead. Roland lived on the sixth-floor, in a modern loft-style penthouse. I gazed out at the bay from his large picture window as he put in our order. While we waited for our food to arrive, he showed us around the place. He had a small gym in the middle of the penthouse, and along the walls were built-in bookshelves packed with books and photographs. Almost all of the pictures were of two women who looked to be his wife and daughter. It seemed like he lived there, alone, though, so I thought maybe his wife had died, and it was her funeral where Roland and Saint last saw each other. Roland next led us outside to a wraparound deck that gave us an incredible panoramic view of the bay, Alameda, and downtown Oakland. It also gave Saint a chance to grab a quick smoke. A half-hour later, we gathered around Roland's dining room table gorging on ribs, brisket, yams, baked beans, macaroni and cheese, and cornbread, with sweet potato pie for dessert.

As we finished our pie, I sat back and listened to the two old friends reminisce. It turned out they knew each other from shore duty in San Diego. Saint had gotten himself into trouble and was in danger of getting kicked out of the service, and Roland, who was the command master chief in charge of the enlisted sailors, went to bat for him. Saint ended up with a light sentence because of Roland's intervention, and he toed the line for the rest of his enlistment.

"That's when I got sober," Saint said. "Jeffries is my Eskimo."

I looked at Roland, confused. He looked back at me, just as confused, and then over at Saint. "You're going to have to explain that one, Chief," he said, motioning to his decidedly non-Inuit black skin.

"It's got nothing to do with igloos," Saint replied. "What I meant was, you're the non-AA guy that led me to AA."

Roland laughed. "Okay, I got you now," he said. Then he explained to me, "My oldest friend goes to AA, and I saw how much it helped him. So, when Saint's back was against the wall, I suggested it to him."

"Still can't thank you enough," Saint humbly said to Roland. Then he abruptly changed the subject. "So, Joppa, Roland owns a law school here in Oakland. We were talking about you recently and thought you might consider applying."

Ah, so this was why Saint asked me to join him in the Bay Area.

"We have a small class that starts in January," Roland told me. "And our admissions policy is open, so don't think you'd be getting in because I did you a special favor or anything."

I'd never considered studying law, and I really had no interest in it at all. I didn't know how to turn down such a kind offer, though — or if I should turn it down, considering I still wasn't sure what to do with myself after leaving the navy. I didn't know what to say, so I just nodded. Roland sensed my apprehension.

"The first year is intimidating and scares a lot of people off, but the second year is actually the hardest, academically. But you survived your first year in the navy, right? This will be a piece of cake compared to that. It could lead to a good career and your GI Bill will cover the cost."

"Okay," I found myself saying. "That sounds great. Thank you for the opportunity!" I guess I was going to law school.

CHAPTER 2

I left San Diego in late December. It was hard to leave the beaches behind, and I had developed a routine with the meetings I was going to, but there wasn't really anything I was tied to there. I'd miss Chris for sure. And while I was close to Oliver, our relationship felt more like family, like we had an obligation to be close because of the sponsorship. I hoped to be more social up in the Bay Area and find some good meetings.

I started classes and moved into the dorms at People's Law right after New Year's Day, along with about thirty other spring admits. In addition to taking a clinical placement, I started classes in civil procedure, legal ethics, contracts, constitutional law, and property. The campus was small, consisting of just a couple buildings that included the classrooms, dorms, cafeteria, offices, and law library, which was open to the public for research.

Officially called the Law Center for the Advancement of the Rights of all People, People's Law was accredited by the state bar of California, but not by the American Bar Association. Someone with a law degree from People's could only take the California bar exam and practice law in the Golden State.

The school had a majority black student population, with a small number of Hispanic, Asian, and white students. At orientation, the admissions director told us the racial makeup of the students, unusual for a law school, was that way by design.

"This school was created to not only promote upward mobility," she explained, "but to also produce more lawyers of color who can serve in their communities, so their neighbors can be represented by someone who understands their culture better than, say, a white middle- or upper-class lawyer might."

During the first week of school, I found a noon meeting nearby in Berkeley that aligned well with my class schedule. After a few days of attending, I recognized someone there from school: Dexter, the operations manager. For the next couple weeks, whenever we saw each other at school or at meetings, we nodded at one another, and after a while, we started chatting. He was super-mellow and chose his words carefully. I enjoyed starting to get to know him and talking to him whenever I could. I quickly saw that he was well-respected by people at meetings and at the school, and I could tell right away that he was going to be an important guide for me here, like Uncle New, Roy, Silver, and Saint had been for me back in Jersey.

I missed those guys and the closeness we'd had. The Bay Area had a lot to offer, but it wasn't home. My world was so small in Oakland. People's Law was in a rough neighborhood, so I didn't leave campus much, except for my increasingly frequent escapes to Berkeley. Mostly, I just hung around the dorm, cafeteria, and library. I was the only white guy in the dorms and I didn't feel like I belonged at all. The other guys never included me in their study groups, or when they smoked weed and drank in the dorms. I was homesick, discouraged, and exhausted. AAs have an acronym for this feeling: HALT, which stands for *hungry*, *angry*, *lonely*, and *tired*. Sober alcoholics don't deal well with these feelings, and their inclination is to reach for a drink. Being aware of and tending to the thing that's bothering you can help you avoid picking up that drink. So, I started to think seriously about moving off campus. The deal was sealed when, at the end of February, my car was broken into and my radio stolen. I knew it was time to go. I realized that moving out might further alienate me from my classmates, but I couldn't worry about that. As Byron used to say, "It's none of my business what others think of me."

At the beginning of March, I rented a room from Dexter in San Rafael, a more upscale city on the other side of the Richmond Bridge from the East Bay, in Marin County. It was about a half-hour for me to get to school, and about the same to get into San Francisco. Dexter rented rooms to a few other people, all of whom were AA members, and it was a sober house, though not a halfway house. The house had been owned by a woman named Delilah James, who was one of the first graduates of People's Law. She was a tough, independent woman, from what I was told, who went to law school after she was done raising her kids and grandkids. She died shortly after passing the bar on her first try, and in her will, she bequeathed the house to the law school. I definitely felt more comfortable living there — being in a sober household with Dexter gave me the positive support and friendship I was missing in the dorms. Plus, there were a lot of AA activities I could participate in there.

Dexter's car was in the shop when I moved in, so he started carpooling with me to the school, and I'd occasionally take him to run errands. One day, we were picking up supplies in Oakland and stopped in at Flint's BBQ. I may not have liked living in Oakland, but you could get some damn good food there. Flint's had just enough room to stand inside to order your food, then you ate on picnic tables outside. Their hours and their menu varied. We were lucky to find them open, and that day ribs, chicken, and brisket were on the menu. We got a big pile of ribs smothered in a dark, sweet and tangy sauce, along with a couple scoops of potato salad, and a few slices of white bread, and enjoyed our meal outside under a big umbrella. Dexter pointed out the 'Til Two, a blues bar he liked to go to, adding "I think alcoholics can hang out in bars if they're there to spend time with friends or listen to music. There are actually quite a few AA members who are bartenders."

I noticed a lot of massage places up and down the street and asked him what the deal was. "Sailors were always talking about going to these places. Are they really a front for prostitution?"

He confirmed what I'd been told. "Yeah, you get a massage and a hand job at those places," he said matter-of-factly without looking up from his ribs. I knew I needed to have stronger ties to AA. I'd moved around a lot since I started in the program, so I didn't have a strong community foundation. I decided to recommit myself by doing a "90 in 90" — 90 AA meetings in 90 days. That would help me get accustomed to the local fellowship, become friendlier with the other attendees, and start building more of a community here. It would become a routine and something I looked forward to each day. I also needed a sponsor, and for this, I turned to Dexter. He'd become sort of a sobriety mentor for me anyway, so we just made it official when I asked him one night and he accepted.

Dexter prayed in the morning and at night, and I got into the habit of doing so as well. He kept his spirituality quiet. It wasn't tied to any eastern or western religion; it mostly came from his dedication to helping people through AA and sobriety. He also got me started on my tenth step inventory. Every night, I reviewed what had happened that day, writing down if I'd been selfish, dishonest, resentful, or fearful, and noting any corrections or amends I needed to make.

Dexter took me to a small noontime meeting in San Rafael one Sunday that was held in the tiny waiting room of a pediatrician's office that was closed for the day. One of the attendees immediately stuck out to me — a cute hippie chick about my age with curly brown hair and glasses. I caught her name when we all introduced ourselves at the beginning of the meeting: Cassandra. I'd be sure to return to that meeting, and look out for her at other meetings in the area.

I also wanted to go deeper into my meditation practice, so I was happy to discover the Berkeley Zen Center on San Pablo. I went to a session after class one day and had a great meditation experience. I'd arrived a little before the session started, so I took off my shoes, found an unoccupied cushion in the meditation room, and settled in. Pretty soon the gong sounded, signaling the start of group meditation. Ten minutes into the sitting, I heard the faint buzzing sound in my ears that meant my mind was calm. As I concentrated on my breathing, I started imagining a broad golden beam of light shining down upon me, feeding me positive energy. I felt safe and at peace, I wished the same for all. This was the best meditation I'd ever experienced. After sitting, we did 10 minutes of walking meditation around the perimeter of the room. As I walked, the golden beam disappeared, but when we sat again, it returned.

A few days later, I went back to the Zen center to have private interview time with Bruno, a Sensei visiting from Sweden. I told him about the golden beam I'd experienced the last time I was there. He smiled and said, "Just keep meditating."

I was confused. He didn't seem to think it was an important moment. "I was really excited about it. Am I being silly?"

"No, no," he replied. "I don't mean to minimize your experience. Remember, though, that the important thing is to keep meditating. You don't want visions like that to be your goal or purpose when you're meditating. You saw the golden beam. Good. Keep meditating. You don't see the golden beam. That's okay, too. Just keep meditating."

CHAPTER 3

Being an unaccredited California law school, People's Law did things differently than most schools. Law school is typically three years, but People's scrapped the third year, which is usually just filled with elective courses. They also tossed the traditional casebook method and instead concentrated on teaching the rules of law in a more straightforward way and training you to do the job and get your license, with lots of bar exam practice. It was almost like a two-year review program for the California bar exam. Students also began interning at clinics within the first few months of entering school, instead of the more traditional approach of getting involved in a clinic in the third year.

My internship began as a small group class with guest lecturers and instruction in dealing with judges and other lawyers, how to interview clients, how to write up complaints, legal research, and ethics training. After six weeks, we chose our internship placements. I went with a victim's rights center located in Fairfax, a beautiful woodsy village near San Rafael. I liked the idea of helping people who had been wronged, rather than busting criminals or working in personal injury law. Plus, the focus of the clinic was assisting those seriously injured by drunk drivers. I committed to six months, volunteering on Monday and Wednesday afternoons. I would be meeting with clients, writing up complaints, and accompanying them in court as they represented themselves.

My internship supervisor, Professor Merkel, also practiced meditation and I'd see him sometimes at the Berkeley Zen Center. As part of my internship requirement, I had to meet with him once a week to discuss my progress and problems, and to ask questions. I enjoyed talking with him. We were only supposed to be discussing my clinical experiences, but I'd find myself chatting with him about everything, and I even shared a bit of my past with him. He had the ability to draw deep thoughts and feelings out of me, and I trusted him completely.

I met Dennis Nishimura, a Japanese-American just a little older than me, in Professor Merkel's class. We were assigned to each other as study partners during midterms. I liked him and started to hang out with him outside of school. He and his wife, Evelyn, lived in an old fourplex in Alameda, a little island south of Oakland that was full of charming Victorians and small-town feel.

Like me, Dennis wasn't really interested in law school. He'd only decided to go so he could avoid working for his father-in-law at one of the family businesses in San Francisco's Japantown. He tended toward anxious, but he'd usually loosen up after a drink, especially once when we got off the topic of law school and onto what we both really loved: baseball. He introduced me to both Bay Area teams, and we started making plans to regularly go to games at the Oakland Coliseum, which was close to Alameda. But, we also had to study. Twice a week we'd head to his place and go over what we'd read, compare notes, and quiz each other.

Dennis had an older brother who lived in San Francisco. We'd go into the city and hang out with him on occasion. One night, we went to his house and had dinner, then the three of us went out to see a band play at Grant & Green in North Beach. I was excited to be hanging out in San Francisco. It reminded me of when I'd go into Manhattan for a big night out. Evelyn met us at the bar that night and brought along her friend Mary Lee. They'd known each other since high school. Mary Lee had gone to Columbia and continued to live in New York for a few years after graduation, so she and I chatted about New York and New Jersey. It felt good to have a normal conversation with a woman outside of AA. And she was really pretty. I hoped I'd get to see more of her.

That night, I crashed on Dennis and Evelyn's couch when we got back to Alameda. It was comfortable, but I woke up early, way before Dennis and Evelyn, and I felt a really strong sexual craving. Hanging out with Mary Lee must have sparked some desire in me that I couldn't shake. I lay there for a moment, thinking about what to do. Let it pass, or go jerk off? But then another idea hit me: the massage parlor. I'd been so curious about them, and I was right by Oakland's Chinatown, which had several parlors. I could sneak away to one and satisfy my curiosity, and my sexual needs.

I quietly got up, got dressed, and went out to my car. As I drove the short distance to Chinatown, I rationalized in my head why this would be okay, kicking the ethical considerations aside. I'd been sober for nearly four years, I'd survived the navy, I'd been studying hard, I'd stayed out of massage parlors all this time — I deserved a reward. But I didn't want this to just be a lustful release. I wanted it to be a spiritual and exploratory moment as well. Maybe I needed to sit in meditation for a minute and get spiritually grounded before embarking on this experience. After I emerged from the Posey Tube, the underwater connector of Alameda and Oakland, I stopped at a pagoda in a nearby park. I sat cross-legged beneath it and tried to clear my mind and get centered. But images of what was to come remained at the forefront of my mind and I couldn't focus on anything but my sexual desire. I gave up on meditating and headed back to my car. I passed by two women who were also meditating and quietly chanting, "Nam myoho renge kyo." I smiled at them, and returning the smile, one of them handed me a card with that same chant on it. On the back was an address in Emeryville and "Wednesdays at 7 pm." I put the card into my wallet, got in my car, and took off toward the nearest massage parlor.

It didn't take long to find one that looked okay. And it had a parking place right out in front. That had to be a sign. I hurried to the door, feeling a mix of shame and nervous excitement. I pulled on the handle, but it didn't open. Then I saw the buzzer. I hit that, and pretty soon I was buzzed in by an elderly, hunched-over Asian woman. I told her I was there for a massage, she took my cash, and then she led me down a hall to a small room. I hoped desperately that she wasn't going to be my masseuse and that I hadn't accidentally wound up in a legit day spa. She told me to sit down, then she left the room, closing the door behind her.

I sat in a chair beside the massage table, looking around the room. There was a white terry cloth robe hanging on a hook on the door — am I supposed to put that on? I was nervous that this was my first time, and that it would show. I had no idea what I was supposed to do other than wait. So I sat there for a few minutes, worrying briefly about a raid by the cops and how embarrassing that would be.

My fears were allayed when an incredibly hot Asian woman opened the door. She was wearing a mini dress with black heels. Her huge tits were practically falling out of her dress, which hugged her perfect ass. She told me to undress, then offered me a shower, which I took. As I toweled off, she instructed me to lie down on the massage table on my stomach, with my face nestled in the head cradle. I looked down at the carpet, and draped a towel over my hairy ass, then I heard the pump of a lotion bottle and she got to business. She massaged my back, neck, and shoulders, loosening muscles that had been tense for so long. My entire body, and my mind, relaxed. I'd pay for this even if it didn't come with a sexual release at the end.

She next massaged my legs and feet. As she worked my hamstrings, her hands softly brushed against my butt cheeks. Then she kneaded my inner thighs, brushing up against my balls. I was hard as a rock and practically dying of anticipation. She told me to turn over, and started massaging my scalp, then worked her way down the sides of my neck to my chest, then my quads. Her strong kneading gradually turned to soft strokes of my inner thighs, where she again brushed up against my balls before directly caressing them. She took my right hand and placed it on her ass. I savored it, stretching my fingertips toward her pussy, then I reached up with my left hand and felt one of her tits just as she grabbed my cock and started stroking. I exploded within seconds. She cleaned me up with a warm towel, then finished with a firm massage of my temples.

I left the parlor, got in my car, and drove back to Alameda with mixed feelings. I felt amazing and satiated, but also guilty and like a loser for having to pay for sex. Most of all, though, I knew in my heart that it needed to be a one-time thing. It felt so good that I already wanted to go back again, and I knew that if I kept it up, I'd be spending every minute possible inside a massage parlor.

CHAPTER 4

I kept up my Marin meetings, always on the lookout for Cassandra, but I never saw her again at the ones I was going to. She had a hold on me — the first cute girl I'd seen at a meeting in a long time. I brought it up to Dexter.

"Oh yeah, Cassandra," he said. "A few AA guys have dated her. She's a member of the speaker meeting down in Sausalito. She sets up before the meetings, and cleans up after."

"Guess I'll be going to Sausalito," I said, smiling. "Thanks for the tip!"

"Well, we'll see if you thank me down the road," he said vaguely, shaking his head. I wasn't sure what he meant, and he didn't explain further, but I chose to ignore that ambiguous comment and made plans to go to the next Sausalito speaker meeting. It was in two days.

Perched on a hillside with incomparable views of the Golden Gate Bridge, the bay, Alcatraz, and San Francisco, Sausalito was much more affluent than San Rafael, and rather touristy. I joined the group, volunteering to be the greeter, with the intention of spending time with Cassandra and getting to know her. In AA, we refer to this as "doing the right thing for the wrong reason." I rationalized this away, telling myself that I needed a commitment and this was a good group.

After a couple weeks of exchanging hellos and small talk, I felt comfortable chatting more and more with Cassandra before and after the meeting. I learned she was a San Francisco native and had ten years of sobriety. We hit it off like I hoped we would, and I asked her out the next week. She said yes and suggested a tour of San Francisco's most iconic neighborhoods.

A few dates in, Cassandra invited me back to her place. She lived in a studio cottage in the back lot of a large Victorian in Mill Valley. She seemed to really have it together, and I admit I was impressed. I was enjoying getting to know her, and especially liked the direction we were headed — kissing and cuddling in her little cottage. After a short while, we started having sex, and it was honestly the best I'd ever had. She had a high sex drive, and we were having sex daily. I was even able to last longer than I ever had.

Suddenly, life felt better than it ever had before. I was falling in love. I felt like I was attaining this ideal I'd been picturing in my head — a relationship with an AA woman, someone I could walk into meetings with, feel proud of, impress people with. I knew we hadn't been dating long, but I started to think that maybe she was the one, even though there were red flags I was dutifully ignoring. She'd judge where I was at in life and mistakes I'd made, but she would never admit mistakes herself. Her sponsor closely monitored everything she did and scrutinized our relationship. So, it wasn't perfect, but it was something and I was all in, totally committed.

On what would be our last date, she took me to the San Francisco Zen Center. How cool! We went inside and looked around, and I vowed to myself that I would one day return to meditate there. In the gift shop, I bought some incense and a beautiful wooden box. Outside, she snapped my picture, which I planned to send to Silver. I was overwhelmed with my feelings, and I impulsively told her how much she meant to me and how good I felt about our relationship. She did not respond, only walked toward her car, and I followed. We rode mostly in silence till we got to her house, and she hurried inside, saying goodbye with a small peck on my cheek.

The next few days, she didn't return my calls, and eventually I stopped calling altogether. I saw her at meetings the next couple weeks, and she was cold. It was over, as quickly as it had begun. I was upset, angry, and felt like a fool. I'd fallen in love immediately, taking it all so seriously, and I thought those feelings were reciprocated. But she was just in it for fun.

I found out later that the house in the front lot of her cottage was actually her parents' and that she lived off them. So she didn't have it as together as I thought. How could I have such strong feelings and rush into something so fast when I hardly knew the girl? I told

Dexter about it, and he shook his head and said, "Yep, that's Cassandra."

"I was head over heels. How did I get it so wrong?"

"Sometimes we want something, some idea of perfection that we have in our head, so badly that we're blind to reality. Just slow down next time — feel your feelings, sit with them and watch them, and when they start to feel overwhelming and like things are too good to be true, meditate on that. Try not to let how you feel carry you away from reality."

Broken hearts so often have bad timing, and mine happened right in the middle of finals in May. I pushed it out of my mind, crammed with Dennis, and took my exams — and actually passed them. I had survived my first semester of law school. Sure, I mostly got Cs, with one B, but I passed.

Dennis and I decided we needed to celebrate. He mentioned the Dragon Disco Palace, a bar on Webster Street, over on the dingier side of Alameda, that he'd passed by but never entered. He felt like having a couple drinks in a lively setting, and we figured with an intriguing name like that, it had to at least be an interesting place. So we headed toward Webster. After grabbing burgers at a place down the street, we walked up to the Dragon Disco Palace and into something entirely unexpected. The bar's clientele included Asian girls dressed like hookers, big black women, rough-looking black dudes, cross-dressers, and drag queens, all living it up on a crowded dance floor. This was certainly lively, and we immediately loved the vibe.

While Dennis tried out a couple different cocktails and I nursed a seltzer with lime, we both came alive in such a joyful atmosphere, letting the stress and boredom from the semester melt away. We had a blast people-watching and chatting and laughing with the other customers. Dennis even danced for a second with a drag queen. We ended up closing the place down, then I drove us back to Dennis' place and we crashed.

The next day, we wanted to go to an A's game, but that morning, on her way out, Evelyn told us she'd made plans for them to visit her friend Mary Lee in Sausalito.

"We'll head up there after I get back from the SGI Center," she said.

At that, Dennis rolled his eyes, and teased her with, "Nam myho renge khyo."

I did a double take as Evelyn shook her head and said, "To each their own. I get something out of it, Dennis."

"Hey, what is that?" I asked. "I heard some ladies in Chinatown chanting that."

I dug around in my wallet and pulled out the card they gave me. Evelyn looked at it and said, "Yeah, that's the place. Why don't you come with me tonight and find out what it is for yourself? I think you'll like it."

She and I drove to a business park in nearby Emeryville, and I followed her into a large office suite. Inside, a small group of people were mingling and chatting. Evelyn explained to me that they meet there every week, chant for 20 minutes, and then discuss Buddhism for about 45 minutes. Pretty soon, we all took seats and began the chant. I'd done very little chanting, and I enjoyed it. The discussion afterward was energetic and thoughtful. I thanked Evelyn afterward.

Though I was glad to have found another Buddhist resource, I was feeling a little adrift, both with my meditation and AA. I'd been attending meetings nightly, but I still hadn't bonded with many people. I had Dennis and Evelyn and Dexter, but I was feeling lonely and like I was spending more time than ever by myself. It was like I needed another outlet, something beyond AA and meditation. A hobby maybe. This is a common feeling in recovery, and it can lead people down bad paths. You can choose to get really into healthy interests, like hiking or other hobbies, but you can also choose to pursue more addictive activities. I decided to make law school my focus for the moment, to avoid going down a negative path that seemed so in reach. My summer semester was going to start just a few weeks after the spring semester ended, and I'd be continuing with my clinic, plus taking some more intensive classes. That should keep my mind busy.

CHAPTER 5

I'd gotten all the way to summer midterms and I was still feeling completely restless. I didn't know what it was, but I had a strong feeling that something needed to happen in my life, and law school wasn't distracting me from that feeling, and neither were AA meetings nor my friendships. I needed to do something. But what?

Since my experience at the massage parlor, I'd been thinking more and more about paying for sex again. It became an obsession, much like my brothel fixation on my road trip when I neared Vegas. Seeking out my next sexual escapade was not only a distraction from my racing mind and boring studies, but the sex itself lessened my stress and alleviated my horniness, if only for a moment.

I'd learned from some of the AA guys and my housemates that the place to find prostitutes in San Francisco was the city's Tenderloin district, and in Oakland, it was along San Pablo Avenue. My school was near San Pablo. I could have talked to any number of people about this, to stop myself from doing this, but I chose not to. I chose, instead, to start looking for hookers on the streets.

While the selection on San Pablo was smaller, I was told there was less competition and fewer cops. I learned quickly that the black girls were cheaper, and actually my preferred type. Especially the bigger ones with huge tits and wide hips. They all had fake names like Cocoa and Sugar. It somehow felt right to be doing this in this bad part of Oakland, with these girls — there was already an air of anonymity and indifference in the neighborhood. I didn't feel judgment from the girls or the people on the streets. I could come to their neighborhood, get my rocks off, and no one in my lily-white world of suburbia would ever know.

The summer semester was short, and not long after midterms, it was time for finals in August. As I handed in my final to Professor Merkel, he asked me to stop by his office later. When I did, I found him sitting at his desk with a serious look on his face. He motioned for me to sit down

"Joppa, look, you're not into this," he said. "You've done a lot of work to get your life together, but we both know law is not your thing. Why not choose something that you're actually passionate about?"

I was shocked. I agreed with him, of course, but I didn't expect one of my professors to say this to me.

He continued, "I never thought I would suggest this to a student, but I think you should consider dropping out before the fall term begins. You can take some time to think about what it is you truly want to do."

"Well, I'd love to," I said. "You're right, this isn't for me. But I'm a little embarrassed at the prospect of dropping out."

"If you do it, you don't have to tell people right away. You have some time before the semester starts. You could think about what you truly want to do, and then tell people closer to when school starts up again, once you've formed a new plan for yourself."

I appreciated hearing this — it's like I was being given permission to do what I truly wanted to do. One of Saint's truisms came back to me: "You can't save your face and your ass at the same time." I'd been saving face by remaining in the law program, but as a consequence, I'd reached new emotional and spiritual lows.

"But I'd still like to meet with you in my office every Monday at 3," he said. "Until you're more settled. And of course, if that becomes a conflict with a new job, just tell me and we can set a new time. Does that work for you?"

"Yeah, that sounds great," I replied. "Thank you. I feel relieved. I couldn't imagine suffering through one more semester of this."

I left Merkel's office and headed to the Nishimuras', where I promptly told them I was dropping out of People's Law. They were both shocked, and Dennis looked a little envious. From there, I went home to San Rafael and told Dexter. He said he'd let me slide on the rent if I helped him fix the house up in my downtime. He was spending more and more time at his girlfriend Loretta's house in Vallejo, as their relationship got more serious, so he needed the help.

The next day, I already had two jobs. A few days before dropping out, I'd noticed a help wanted sign in the window of the New York–style pizza joint down the street from the house. I stopped in the day after my meeting with Merkel and applied, telling them about my delivery experience. They hired me on the spot. And Evelyn was able to get me in with the temp agency where she worked as a receptionist. They had available placements for office work and manual labor, and since I was able to start immediately, they assigned me to jobs right away. Delivering pizzas was okay. I appreciated the spending money, but I didn't fit in with my coworkers, and that made it a lot less fun. I also felt a little embarrassed, especially when I delivered to people my age who seemed to be successful and happy with their lives. Over the next six weeks, the temp agency sent me to Alameda to help clean out a dive shop that was closing its doors, then to Hayward to record payments made on mortgages for a bank, and then to San Leandro to do some filing in an office. I was also tasked with delivering photocopiers all around the East Bay. Assignments could last anywhere from four hours to three weeks, and between that and delivering pizzas a couple nights per week, time was flying by.

During this transitional time, I was also making sure to maintain my social and spiritual life: hanging out with the Nishimuras, meeting with Merkel every week, going to meetings, and meditating at the Berkeley Zen Center. I was also exercising a lot and getting out and exploring the Bay Area. Dexter and I worked on remodeling the house, and I was really enjoying hanging out there with my housemates. I set up the TV room just in time for us to watch the Los Angeles Dodgers play the Oakland A's in the World Series. The moment I decided to drop out, I felt an immense sense of relief. This lasted for several weeks, slowly dwindling, until the novelty of my new situation wore off, and then I felt down again. Here I was, a sober navy vet in his late-twenties, with no direction. I tried to work through these feelings of disappointment and aimlessness. I did my gratitude lists, acknowledging all that I had to be grateful for. And there was a lot. But I still felt like there wasn't enough in my life — of anything — and I didn't know how to fill that hole.

CHAPTER 6

Dexter's and my sober birthdays were in October — my fourth, his twenty-fifth— so we decided to throw a joint party for ourselves with our friends and the guys from the house. We had a barbeque at China Camp, a park along San Pablo Bay, and Dexter and I got there early to set up. As Dexter unpacked the car, I got the two grills at our picnic spot going. I was concentrating on lighting the charcoal in the second grill when I heard a car door slam. I looked up, and I did a double take. There was Saint, walking toward me from the parking lot — I had no idea he was coming out for this! And he was with Roland, who was walking with an arm around Dexter.

"Happy birthday, Joppa," Saint called out. I met him halfway and gave him a big hug.

"Saint! Thanks for coming out to celebrate. I had no idea."

"Surprised?" Dexter said to me, glancing over at Roland.

"Remember that first night we met, and I mentioned seeing how much AA had helped my oldest friend, so I recommended it to Saint?" Roland said to me. I nodded. "Well, that oldest friend is Dexter here."

Ah, I didn't put that together and Dexter never let on. I couldn't have been happier to see Saint, and I was excited to see Roland, too. Saint helped me on the grills, and more people started to show up. First some of the guys from the house, then a few regulars from my Sausalito AA home group and some of Dexter's buddies from the Berkeley noon meeting, and finally Dennis and Evelyn with Mary Lee.

I was happy to see Mary Lee again. It was fun to talk to her that first night I met her, and out here in the sunlight, I could see that she was even prettier than I'd already thought. I noticed her looking at me from time to time as I manned the grill, so once I was free, I made my way over to her and we chatted for a long time. I found out that she was actually 10 years older than me, and that she'd been married before. We also talked a little more about her time in New York. She was great to talk to — so smart and funny, and just genuinely classy. I liked her.

Saint came over to us, then turned toward the rest of the party, put his fingers in his mouth, and whistled. The chatting came to a halt, as everyone focused on Saint.

"I just want to honor my good friend Joppa here," he said. "He's come a long way and done a great job. I couldn't be prouder."

Then he presented me with his four-year coin. I was so touched. Everyone clapped as I held back tears.

Roland stood up and put an arm around Dexter, and talked about their childhood together, Dexter's journey through sobriety, and how he was truly his best friend. At that point, everyone was choked up, and the two men embraced. Mary Lee stood up and clapped, and everyone else joined her. Soon, we were all talking over each other and laughing and the party was back in full swing. I kept chatting with Mary Lee, every now and then catching Evelyn's approving glance from across the way. What a fun party — truly one of the best times I'd had in sobriety.

The party wound down and Saint gave me one last hug. He and Roland drove off, waving out the window at me and Dexter. The two of us packed up the car, not saying much. I was reflecting on the day and how grateful I felt in that moment. Where would I be in another four years, I wondered. We finished loading the car and when Dexter slammed the trunk closed, we both noticed a sailboat off in the distance near San Quentin. We stopped to watch it for a few seconds.

"I don't know much about sailing," Dexter said, "but I heard once that if you're in trouble at sea and the wind is tossing you about, it's best to just take your hands off the tiller and let the wind blow your boat the way it's supposed to go."

CHAPTER 7

My next temp assignment was at a title company in Alameda, where I was working as a proofreader in a typing pool of about a dozen ladies. The work was steady and in a nice environment, but there was one problem: the head of the department, Lucille. She was a big Portuguese girl in her early thirties with huge, round breasts, wide hips, a small waist, thick curly brown hair, and a perfect ass. She wore lots of perfume, tight skirts, and low-cut blouses. And she sat right across from me. It was torture.

She could be a little pushy, which only made her sexier to me. I was already horny all the time, and she just pushed me over the edge. Every day, all day long, I was bombarded with those tits and that ass. My dick was permanently half-hard, and though I was getting my work done, my thoughts were constantly returning to her body. As soon as I got home from work every day, I'd jerk off like a man possessed.

I liked to read the *Chronicle* on my lunch breaks, and one day I noticed ads in the sports section for strip shows at the Market Street Cinema in downtown San Francisco. Pretending to be reading about the latest baseball game, I was instead absorbed in an ad that featured a dancer with "boobs the size of basketballs." I had to see those. After finishing up at the title company, then delivering pizzas for a few hours, I headed to the city to catch the 10 pm show.

The theater was as sleazy as I imagined it would be. Girls were swarming all over the place giving guys lap dances, while other women danced on the stage. It reminded me of the time my cousin Dan and I snuck into a dirty movie when I was 13 and he was 14. We thought it would be funny, but as soon as we got into the theater, we were just grossed out by the guys sitting inside — what a bunch of perverts, we thought. We left pretty quickly and stopped by the bathroom on our way out. Inside, there was a guy drying the crotch of his pants with the hand dryer. We realized this meant he'd blown a load in his pants, and we were doubly grossed out. Like, how pathetic can a guy get?

And now I was that guy. I knew it, but that wasn't enough to stop me from sitting right at the front of the stage, eagerly waiting for the featured dancer to come out. And there she was, just as advertised. Her tits were absolutely gigantic, and I was instantly erect as she started dancing. She stripped down to a bright-red sequined G-string with matching pasties, then strutted back and forth across the edge of the stage, cupping her boobs and shaking them in our faces. I reached for my wallet, pulled out a ten dollar bill and stuck it in her sweaty cleavage. She grabbed my hand and placed it on her left breast, letting me grab at it as she blew me a kiss. Then she strutted offstage and was gone.

I looked around at the girls working the floor and decided I should get a lap dance. I caught an older redhead's eye, and she sauntered over to me and sat her naked ass on my lap. She turned her head to look back at me and held out a hand. "Presents?" she said in her cutesiest voice. Part of me was as grossed out as I had been in that dirty movie theater as a teenager, but a more insistent part of me was pulling out a wad of bills and placing them in her hand. I felt a sense of urgency — I needed this, right now. She curled her fist around the bills, and started bouncing and grinding on me. It didn't take long for me to come, and then she was up and on to the next customer. I was completely satiated for the moment, and also disgusted with myself. I could see the wet stain forming on the crotch of my pants.

Back at the office the next day, I was as horny as ever. The visit to the strip club the night before did nothing to assuage this unending lust. And Lucille's tits didn't help. I went through the motions at work, then when I got off, I'd cruise San Pablo on my way home to Marin. This became an everyday thing — something I looked forward to, like I used to look forward to partying. I'd drive up and down the different streets I knew the hookers usually hung out on, my eyes darting left and right, looking for girls and for cops at the same time. Even when a street seemed deserted, if you gave it a moment, a girl would pop up — they were always there, finishing a trick, and then back on the sidewalk ready for the next guy. As soon as I'd turn my car in that direction, it was like I became a different person. I was crazed, controlled by feelings of lust and anticipation. The hunt and the risk involved made my adrenaline surge. That feeling was almost better than the moment in the front seat that would come a little later: grabbing at giant tits while getting jerked off.

Trolling for whores became my new hobby and my new addiction, I suppose. It was an escape from everyday life, and it shook things up. In AA, they say that alcoholics are prone to feeling restless, irritable, and discontented. I'd certainly been feeling that way, and this new hobby gave me something to do, something to think about other than the disappointment I felt about my job situation. It also introduced an element of danger that I was missing from no longer partying. I knew I was up to no good, because I kept my actions from Dexter for a long time. Usually, you run things by your sponsor — and when you don't, it's because you know you're doing the wrong thing, and they'll hold you accountable. You might tell another friend from AA, but only someone who you know would say it's no big deal. We'd call that "co-signing bullshit."

But I did finally tell Dexter what I was up to. He seemed neither shocked nor disappointed, which made me feel a little better.

"Our shortcomings don't usually go away completely in AA," he said. "The best you can do is to be aware of them, diminish them, and keep them in check."

We talked about ways I could get my mind off it and do something positive instead. He suggested I keep up with my daily tenth step inventories, share honestly with the guys in AA who I trusted, including him, and make sure to pray and meditate regularly.

"Healing is a combination of God and time," he told me. "Besides, that shit will kill you. You know that expression about filling the void of an alcoholic — it's a bottomless pit. You can never get enough."

CHAPTER 8

Despite talking to Dexter about my trolling, I kept it up. It had a strong hold over me. I was feeling so bad about it, and yet I was still doing it. I realized that I was no longer following God's will, but instead following my own, which was bound to get me into trouble. I no longer felt proud of myself, and like I was doing the right thing. I lost my confidence and felt like I'd never be able to diminish any of my shortcomings. Was I doomed? In AA, we're told not to beat ourselves up when we fall short, and that we seek progress and not perfection. I was beating myself up, but continuing the behavior. What would my bottom be? Did I have a bottom?

One Friday night on San Pablo, I got caught. I was in my car with a hooker, and a cop shined her flashlight inside. The girl jumped out of my car and took off, and the cop let me go with a warning. I'd have hoped that scare would've been my bottom, but it wasn't. I was back out two days later, after brunch with Dennis and Evelyn.

They'd invited me to Alameda to hang out with them overnight that Saturday. We had dinner and played games, and it was really fun and relaxing. It felt good to be with them, talking about work and school and life. I told them I was feeling anxious about not knowing where my life was headed. Evelyn pointed out that I was happy living at Dexter's and working on the house with him, and encouraged me to keep the faith that things would fall into place soon. The phone rang, and Evelyn excused herself to answer it. As she chatted in the other room, Dennis told me that he didn't know how much longer he could take law school. We talked quietly about it until Evelyn came back in.

"That was Mary Lee," she said, with a scheming smile. "Tony, she wanted me to tell you hi."

The next morning, we went to Ole's Waffle Shop in Alameda for brunch. I was happy hanging out with them, but a nagging feeling was distracting me. I knew when brunch was over, I needed to leave. I needed to get to Oakland. I made up an excuse to go home, and, after we said our goodbyes and I got in my car, I headed straight to San Pablo. I didn't even try to fight it. The streets were empty as I rolled through — it was Sunday morning after all. But I knew they were out there somewhere. They always are. I drove around a bit longer, and then I spotter her: Bubblicious, one of my favorites of the big-breasted girls. She was standing near the AME church, wearing a black leotard that was so tight and so low, her huge tits spilled halfway out over the top.

I called her over to my car, and just as she was about to get in, people from the neighborhood began filing out of the church. There was no hiding what we were up to, and the group of churchgoers was outraged. This was their neighborhood, after all, and here I was with a hooker on a beautiful Sunday morning, right in front of their church. They surrounded my car and shouted at me. I was scared they were going to drag me out and beat me up, when the crowd parted and a cop appeared by my car. I was relieved at first, but the next minute, I was being arrested for soliciting a prostitute. Bubblicious was arrested, as well.

I spent the night in jail. I felt completely defeated. There was nothing I could do in that cell but think and pray. Instead of asking for mercy, I prayed for God's will and the power to carry it out. I was somehow able to fall asleep, and when I woke up the next morning, I felt more at ease, like everything would be all right and the worst was over. I saw a judge that morning, and she gave me my car back and set my trial for that Friday.

When Friday rolled around, I sat in the lobby at the municipal court in Oakland, waiting for my case to be called. Just my luck, students from People's Law were there that day with Professor Kern to observe cases. Not everyone knew I'd dropped out, so for a while, it seemed like most of the students assumed I was there for the same reason they were. That of course changed when my case was called. We all filed into the courtroom, but as they took seats in the gallery, I continued through the gate and took my place in front of the judge. I imagine they were shocked, but I didn't turn to see. I was too embarrassed.

Bubblicious was also there, wearing only slightly more than what she'd been dressed in when I solicited her. She was also representing herself. As the proceedings began, she told the judge that I was a friend, referring to me as "Honey Boy," and that I had just pulled over to say hello. I heard stifled laughter behind me. The judge clearly did not believe the story — no one in that courtroom did — but because no one had witnessed money being exchanged, he dropped our case and we were excused. I turned to leave, and Bubblicious was suddenly by my side, linking arms with me. We walked out together — she giggled, while I looked straight ahead, avoiding the stares of my former classmates. I was relieved, but mortified.

When I got home, I went straight to my room, avoiding Dexter. I'd completely disregarded the advice he'd given me and I was embarrassed. I needed to talk to someone about it, though. Just not someone who was my sponsor — not yet anyway. So I called Byron. I knew he'd be nonjudgmental and make me laugh. He got a kick out of my trial, and by the end of our conversation, I was able to joke about it, too.

"You gotta tell Dexter, though," he told me. "He's your sponsor and he'll help you. If you're not comfortable telling him, then you need to consider if he's the right sponsor for you. And if he's not, you need to get a new one before you relapse completely."

Dexter was a great sponsor. My reluctance to tell him about what happened was rooted in my disappointment with myself, and not from a fear of how I thought he might react. I knew he'd be supportive. I sat in my room for a few minutes after hanging up with Byron and breathed slowly and deeply. Then I got up and found Dexter.

He wasn't surprised by anything I told him. "I'm sorry you didn't talk to me about it as you were going through it, but I'm glad you're telling me now. Why don't you do a fourth step inventory of your behavior, see what you come up with."

"I will," I replied. "I think this was my bottom. I haven't felt so low since the last time I was arrested, sitting in a holding cell. I can't believe I spiraled out of control like this. What the fuck happened?"

"The trolling is just a substitution for drinking," he said. "You can take comfort, though, knowing that if this was your bottom, things are only going to go up from here. It'll be hard work, but you've done it before. And you can do it again."

"I've got to find a better work situation. I'm so dissatisfied and bored all day long. Could I do more here to help out with management?"

"I've been talking to Roland about this, actually," Dexter said. "With the house owned by the school, and with so many students coming through here, he and I talked about making this one of the school's official off-campus housing facilities. It would be a men's-only sober house, like it is now, but just for People's Law students. There are a lot of guys at that school who need a place like this. Which leads me to you. Loretta and I are planning on moving in together soon, so I'll be relocating to Vallejo in the next month or so. We'll need a new manager here, and I hoped you'd be interested. You'd get to stay here, manage the place, and help newly sober students out. Roland has some ideas for other aspects of the job that he wants to talk to you about, if you're interested."

"Are you kidding? That's perfect! Yes, of course, that's exactly what I want to do."

Things were looking up already. The next day, I met with Roland to go over the details about my new position and to sign paperwork making it official. He wanted me to do more than just manage the house; he also wanted me to be the school's community resource liaison for students interested in getting sober, and to help students with legal issues get those affairs in order before sitting for the bar. I was really excited about this opportunity. I was also embarrassed, because I knew word about my case had gotten around fast at the school. Roland didn't judge me. He just told me to keep working the steps and to stick with Dexter. "I think this new job will have a very positive effect on you, Tony."

When I left Roland's office, I stopped by Professor Merkel's. The moment I walked in, he gave me a look that told me he also knew. He shook his head and grinned, then quoted Oscar Wilde, "There is only one thing in life worse than being talked about, and that is not being talked about."

I chuckled sheepishly.

"Relax, Joppa, you're human. It was just an issue you needed to work through. You've become your own man now — you're figuring things out for yourself. So you dropped out of school and then got arrested. Think you're the first person to do that? You're just finding your way. Remember, the Buddha himself was the world's greatest dropout. He had a kingdom lined up, but instead went off to go sit by a fig tree."

He then held out his hand. "Anyway, I want to welcome you on board. It'll be great to work with you!" We shook hands, chatted a bit more, and then I left to head home and call the pizza parlor and temp agency to tell them I had found full-time, permanent employment.

Life is certainly cyclical, full of highs and lows. Once again, I'd felt at my lowest, and then was presented with a new, positive situation. I was learning that there really is no constant, and no point where I'll have things all figured out. I'll just keep growing with every challenge.

CHAPTER 9

I began shadowing Dexter immediately, learning everything I needed to know to be the live-in manager at the newly dubbed *Delilah James Sober Students Dormitory*, or, as we all took to calling it, *Delilah House*. As he started to move his stuff to Loretta's, I took over his bedroom and began interviewing students for admittance to the house. The few residents who had no connection to the school were given time to relocate, and Dexter and I helped them as much as we could with finding other sober houses in the area. There were a few things I needed to do for the liaison part of my job. I needed to earn a California drug and alcohol counselor certification through a program that was taught by local Narcotics Anonymous members. Then I needed to attend a seminar in San Diego in July that focused on working as a campus liaison for sober housing. I also joined addiction counseling and campus administration professional organizations.

This was the first job I'd ever had that made me happy and gave me a feeling of fulfillment. I was so pleased to be able to do something as important as aiding these students who were in a similar position as I was, and who maybe just needed a kind helping hand. I worked on campus a few hours every day during the week. I met Professor Merkel for meditation in Berkeley most mornings before work, and Dexter and I carpooled together to our daily noon AA meetings.

I actually liked being on campus now that I was no longer taking classes there. Dexter's office was right next to mine, and Dennis and I could get together at the end of the day a few times a week.

We caught up during my first week on the job. After settling in at the nearby card room for some corned beef sandwiches, he told me about his continued struggles with school and I told him about my new job. Then he told me something that made my stomach jump.

"Mary Lee wants you to ask her out," he said, passing me her phone number. "Evelyn will kill me if you don't at least give her a call."

I called her that night. We ended up talking for four hours, and made plans to hike at Muir Woods the next day. She was so out of my league, but for whatever reason, she liked me, and we clicked right away. I was going to try not to mess this up.

Things moved quickly with Mary Lee. After that first hike, we started seeing each other just about every day. I thought about Cassandra and how fast that relationship had escalated, and then fizzled, but this situation felt different. It felt like it was headed somewhere real and long-lasting. She got me and she didn't judge me.

Mary Lee was studying for her CPA exam, so we spent a lot of nights in with me quizzing her. We also hung out with Dennis and Evelyn a lot. It felt great to be part of a twosome, instead of the perennial third-wheel. We spent Christmas with them in Alameda, and then they came up to Sausalito for New Years' Eve where we watched the fireworks with the Golden Gate Bridge and the San Francisco skyline as our backdrop. I had my arm around Mary Lee as the fireworks went off and we kissed at midnight. How had I gotten so lucky?

Spring semester began a couple of weeks after New Year's, and there I was, counseling students, holding meetings, and making phone calls. I added more Dockers, dress shirts, and ties to my wardrobe, and I even bought two suits and some aftershave. I'd made a big leap from overgrown college kid to working professional, and I couldn't help but feel a little bit like an imposter. Professor Merkel encouraged me, telling me I'd earned it and I'd grow into the role. Roland gave me a brass navy medallion to hang in my office, and my mother sent me my framed Monmouth degree. I was set to receive my drug and alcohol counseling credential in March, which I'd also hang in my office. I was meeting a lot of new people with my work, from attorneys at the California Bar Committee to addiction counselors, and I began to build a solid professional network.

I was really enjoying meeting with the students who needed addiction help. During our appointments, I'd assess their needs, match them up with the appropriate recovery program, and go over other resources that could help them. The second floor of the dorm on campus was reserved for sober housing, and that's where all the women in the sober program lived, in addition to the men who were not at *Delilah House*. I met with the men in the program every Sunday morning for breakfast at Ole's Waffle Shop in Alameda, and with the women on Friday afternoons in the moot courtroom.

By February, I'd filled up *Delilah House* with a good group of guys. The incoming residents were newcomers to AA and they saw me as an expert, asking me all kinds of questions about the program and the steps. I realized that I was kind of the Saint of that house. We started a meditation meeting, inviting other locals to join us on Saturday afternoons for ten minutes of silent meditation followed by a discussion. My schedule was packed with my office hours, credential class, meetings, working with the sober students, and *Delilah House*. Plus, I was seeing Mary Lee as often as I could. She'd taken and passed her CPA exam around the time school started. All in all, I was feeling great, for the first time in — well, maybe for the first time ever.

CHAPTER 10

With my first semester of work under my belt, I decided it was time for a trip home. I was excited to see everyone, but I also still felt shame around dropping out and about my arrest and spiral into buying sex. I'd told my mom about quitting school when I made the decision, and she didn't say much, which I took to mean she was disappointed in me. I hadn't told anyone but Byron about the hookers. I talked to Dexter about all this as he drove me to the airport, and he reassured me.

"Are you kidding? You're going home like a champ. You've completely turned your life around. Nobody's going to care that you quit law school when you have a job that's meaningful to you and that you enjoy. Plus, you've got a great girl."

As I took my seat on the plane, I reviewed my eighth step list that I'd put in my jacket pocket the night before. It was time to do my ninth step, that is, to make amends to people back in Jersey.

My mother picked me up at the airport in Newark, and I started with my amends right away. I told her I was sorry for all the worrying I'd caused her and for being so ungrateful in the past. She burst into tears, thanking me and telling me she never felt like I owed her an apology. She was happy for me — happy that

I'd found a place where I felt like I belonged and that I'd turned things around. That night, I took my mother and Uncle New out to dinner at our favorite seafood place, the Clam Broth House in Hoboken. Later, back at my mom's condo, I tried to make amends to New, but he waved me off and said basically the same things my mom had said. He was happy for me and I had nothing to apologize for.

The next morning, I went over to Last House to see Saint and the boys. Byron was laid up with the flu, so I was only able to chat with him for a few minutes. Saint invited me to join him and the other guys at an AA conference that afternoon in New Brunswick. I sat up front in the van with Saint as we drove up there, and spending time with him reminded me of how far I'd come since we'd first met. He told me how proud he was of my progress. After the conference, I stopped by Skinny Vinnie's to say hi to Roy before heading back up to my mother's in Hoboken. I didn't get to see Jon, but we had a long phone conversation. In the end, I felt good about myself. I'd made amends and got to experience life with my friends and family as a better-functioning version of myself. I was now experiencing the rewards of doing things the right way, and it felt good. I liked being back in Jersey, but I realized that it was no longer home. California was home now, and I was looking forward to getting back there.

A couple months after my trip to Jersey, People's Law flew me down to San Diego for the sober housing liaison training. I'd only be there for a few days, so I looked up Chris right away when I got there. We met at Balboa Park and caught up, then made plans to spend the Fourth of July together at his and Becky's place. After the last day of the conference, I called Mary Lee from my hotel room.

"Tony," she said, sounding serious, but excited, "I'm pregnant."

I was speechless for a second, but then blurted out, "What?! I'm gonna be a dad? That's awesome!"

Then I added, "Let's get married!"

She said yes, and added, "I've already found a house for us to move into in the same neighborhood as *Delilah House*."

I asked her to fly down to San Diego so we could celebrate, and then we planned to drive back to Marin together, with a stop at a wedding chapel in Vegas on the way. She arrived on the Fourth of July, and after picking her up in my rental car, we drove to Chris and Becky's in Chula Vista. I introduced them to Mary Lee, chuckling to myself as I remembered what had happened the last time I'd invited a woman to their house. Then I blurted out our big news. Becky squealed and Chris gave me a huge bear hug. He and I hung around the barbeque, talking and laughing, while Becky and Mary Lee chatted at the picnic table under the umbrella. It was a beautiful day.

When we finished our dinner, Chris drove us all over to Ocean Beach to watch the fireworks. The place was a madhouse, with people and cars everywhere. We couldn't park anywhere near the pier, so we dropped off the girls and looked for parking. We ended up finding a spot about a mile away, up the hill, practically in Point Loma. As we parked, Chris pulled a big bag of marshmallows out from the center console. I wasn't sure what those were for, and I gave him a funny look. "You'll see," he replied

When we got back to the pier, we found the girls and wedged our way into the crowd by a jetty to watch the show. The sun went down and the fireworks began booming away, filling the sky with lights and color. At the same time, a marshmallow fight broke out among the huge crowd. Apparently, this was a local tradition — and it was fun as hell. After the fireworks, we crashed at Chris and Becky's, and in the morning, they insisted on following us to Vegas to witness our wedding ceremony. We now had a matron of honor and best man.

CHAPTER 11

By the time fall semester started, Mary Lee was four months pregnant. She had completed all the CPA tests and requirements, her business was off the ground in Sausalito, and we'd moved into that place in San Rafael near *Delilah House*, which she spent a lot of time decorating. Dennis and Evelyn helped us fix the place up and the four of us continued to spend a lot of time together.

I checked in on *Delilah House* every day, just to make sure things were going okay with the guys and the house itself, and I'd usually sleep there once a week. Dennis liked to come with me sometimes. We'd hang out with the guys, some of whom Dennis knew from school, and catch a baseball game with them in the TV room. Dennis would be graduating soon and his brother had lined him up with a job as a lawyer at his realty company.

I continued my regular meetings in Marin and Berkeley. My life had become much fuller outside of AA, but I still made it a priority and had become much more involved in commitments, like chairing the Sausalito meeting, working the Marin AA phone line, and sponsoring one of my *Delilah House* tenants.

And baseball was back in my life in full force. We watched the playoffs religiously at *Delilah House*, especially excited that the San Francisco Giants and the Oakland A's had a chance to face each other in the World Series. And then they did! We were all so excited — everyone in the Bay Area was excited. Loyalties were divided from North to South, East to West. San Rafael, like much of Marin, tended to root for the Giants, while the East Bay preferred the A's. A few of us tried to get tickets to one of the games, but they quickly sold out or were too expensive. We'd have to be content watching it on our little TV.

Then, right before game three started, the series was interrupted by the biggest earthquake in the Bay Area since the great quake of 1906. Damage was patchy around the Bay. An elevated freeway in Oakland and part of the Bay Bridge collapsed, and the Marina area in San Francisco was heavily affected, but most other areas were okay, especially up in Marin. The most severely damaged area in San Rafael was the Canal, a working-class Mexican neighborhood built on landfill. The residents had few resources, so the community came together to help out after the quake, bringing our neighbors food, getting them to hospitals, finding lost pets, cleaning up debris, and simply showing that we cared. *Delilah House* volunteered in the Canal area as well as in San Francisco.

The day before the World Series was to resume, one of our residents, Juan Carlos Saliva, who we called Spit, said he had an in at Candlestick Park and he could get all of us at *Delilah House* into the next game for free. That game was to take place on October 27, my fifth sober birthday, and I couldn't think of a better way to celebrate.

That day, we rented a big van to accommodate the *Delilah House* guys, me, Mary Lee, Dennis, Evelyn, Roland, and Dexter. As everyone was getting inside, Dexter motioned me over to his car. He reached into the driver's side window and pulled out an AA birthday card he'd made out to me, a five-year AA coin, and a purple velvet Crown Royal bag that clinked when he handed it to me. He gave me a hug, and then noticed the confused look on my face as I looked down at the Crown Royal bag.

"Open it up," he said. There was a bunch of marbles inside. "Now that you have five years, you've got your marbles back. When you get ten years, I'll explain to you how to use them." I laughed and gave him a hug, then we piled into the van with everyone else.

You'd think we were kids on our way to Disneyland. We were laughing and singing all the way down to Candlestick. Roland was wearing an old Reggie Jackson jersey and Dexter had on a Willie Mays jersey. They were kidding and punching each other in the arm like a couple teenagers.

When we got to the stadium, pulling up to a security guard at a maintenance entrance, Spit hung his head out the passenger side window and called out, "Danny!"

The security guard beamed and walked over to give Spit a high five. "Spit, come on back! You guys can park here, and then head up into the stands."

We didn't have seats, so we just had to roam around Candlestick Park, watching from whatever empty seats we could find, standing in the aisles, or leaning on the railings. That didn't matter — it was the thrill of a lifetime. And what an amazing game! The A's hit five homers, including two by Dave "Hendu" Henderson and one by swaggering Jose Canseco. The Giants answered back with two home runs as well, one by Matt Williams. But the A's won the day, the win going to the starter, Dave Stewart, his second one of the series. The announcers noted that all those homers made it a record-setting World Series game — seven total home runs in a game was a record itself, and the five by the A's alone tied a record set by the 1928 Yanks. The A's would win the fourth game the next day, sweeping the series. I was happy about that — I considered the East Bay to be the "Jersey side" of the Bay Area, and, every so often, the Billy Martins of the world needed to come out on top.

As we drove home, I looked out the window. The 1980s would soon give way to the 1990s. I thought about where I'd started, and where I was now. Twenty years ago, I was a carefree baseball-obsessed kid who had a lifetime of possibilities ahead of him. Ten years ago, at the start of the '80s, I was almost 20 years old, drinking and smoking and going nowhere. Five years ago, I was in jail for drunk driving and selling weed.

And that night, I was that baseball-obsessed kid again, with a lifetime of possibilities ahead of me, happily watching the World Series with my pregnant wife and friends by my side. Out of addiction, depression, and depravity, I had created a new life for myself, one full of promise.

Two months after the World Series, on Christmas Day, my old hero Billy Martin died, in a drunk driving crash. That could have been me.

One Man's Journey
from Self-Destruction to Self-Realization

ABOUT THE AUTHOR

David Jones was born and raised in New Jersey. He briefly worked in the media field in and around New York City after college, and then moved to California for a few years before heading back East to attend law school in Delaware.

While practicing law in his home state of New Jersey, David joined the U.S. Naval Reserve and liked it so much that he quit his job at the law firm and got into active duty.

During his six years in the navy, David earned a Master's Degree in Counseling, and now counsels teens in Las Vegas, Nevada, where he lives with his wife, Reneé.

When not busy with work, David enjoys time with family, hiking, meditating, kayaking, and traveling. His eclectic experiences served as a springboard for this novel, **An Ocean of Thoughts: One Man's Journey from Self-Destruction to Self-Realization**.

CPSIA information can be obtained
at www.ICGtesting.com
Printed in the USA
FSHW010144270921
85035FS